EPISODES OF THE
REVOLUTIONARY WAR

Episodes

of the

Revolutionary War

by ERNESTO CHE GUEVARA

INTERNATIONAL PUBLISHERS
New York

Originally Published in Spanish as
Pasajes de la Guerra Revolucionaria,
Ediciones Unión, Havana, 1963

First Edition

Library of Congress Catalog Card Number: 68–19920
Manufactured in the United States of America

Editor's Preface

Guerrilla Major Ernesto Che Guevara, on October 8, 1967, at the age of 39, was wounded in battle in the Bolivian mountains and taken prisoner. On the following day, in Quebrada del Yuro, he was murdered by the military tyrants, in the presence of CIA personnel.

The legendary hero can hardly be called an Argentinian (although he was born one on June 14, 1928) or a Cuban, although he enjoyed the unusual distinction of having been granted full citizenship by the Revolutionary Republic, where he commanded deep love and high office. He was rather one of those universal men—like Tom Paine or Simon Bolivar—who called his own any country whose people fought tyranny and oppression. As a young man of 26, fully equipped by family position and education to practice the profession of medicine, he joined the resistance forces in Guatemala in their vain attempt to save the only popular democratic government of the Americas from the CIA-sponsored counter-revolution.

From this defeat he wandered to Mexico, convinced that all Latin countries faced a common enemy, the imperialism of the North sustained by local tyrannies, and that this oppressive force would have to be met by the force of the people, by revolutionary force. Later, in retrospect, he confessed to some romanticism in the service of a noble idea when he joined Fidel Castro and his fellow Cuban revolutionists and embarked with them from Mexico on the fateful *Granma* expedition. Che's own vivid story of the first disastrous encounter in the cane-fields near the lonely beach shows that whatever romantic illusions remained after the *Granma* crossing must have vanished on the spot. Out of the initial group of 83, Che was one of the 15 or so who managed to find each other in the Sierra Maestra.

How this small band within a few months was transformed into a Rebel Army is told in these pages. The *Episodes* start with the baptism of fire at that first, almost fatal battle in December 1956, when Che thought for certain he was dead, and cover the eight months during which the Rebel Army took shape in the Sierra. The four articles which have been added as an appendix place this crucial formative period in the context of the entire war. In them, Che tells of the invasion of the plains in 1958 that culminated in the fall of the city of Santa Clara—the decisive battle of which Che was chief strategist— leading to the flight of dictator Fulgencio Batista and the victory of the Revolution on January 1, 1959.

Although the account is devoted almost entirely to the actions in which Che participated, it offers a remarkable picture of the life, mores and battles of the initial guerrilla forces. Che tells the story with great candor, even at his own expense, shunning the heroic pose or glorification of men and events, with almost deliberate understatement and immense modesty about his own role. He writes of the brilliant strikes and the setbacks, the heroes and the renegades, the planned and the accidental, the tragic and the ludicrous. With complete integrity and devotion to the historic undertaking, he seeks authenticity, without distortion or exaggeration. From this simply told, honest story, the truly heroic and historic emerges in the very telling, as in a work of art. The rebel soldiers themselves, the peasant guides and providers, raw recruits from the cities, the emmissaries that come and go between the Sierra and the Movement on the plains—all the components of the revolutionary wave are present in these pages, together with the human failings and mistakes of conception and of deed.

There is little of ideology or generalization in this story of Che's. He tells it how it was, at this early stage of the Revolution, democratic and anti-imperialist. In little more than two years after the overthrow of the Batista regime and under the necessity of beating back the Yankee onslaught, it was to become a Socialist Revolution.

To keep the *Episodes* in proper perspective, it must be remembered that Che was not attempting a complete history of the Cuban armed struggle, but only an account of his own direct experience within one sector of that struggle, in the hope that these sketches would encourage others to add to the historic record. The *Episodes* are therefore a contribution to the history of the early guerrilla phase of the Revolution. Furthermore, to explain how that small guerrilla band acted as the spark for the first successful socialist revolution in the Americas, it would be necessary to go beyond the events described in this book. The Revolution as a whole would have to be studied to discern its specific quality and to distinguish what is unique to it and what is universal, or even what may be common to Latin America.

The present book reveals only one rich aspect of Che's extraordinary personality. He was a fully endowed revolutionary man, in whom the guerrilla strategist and fighter embodied a dynamic Marxist outlook. He left many writings which show his eager search for fresh theoretical insights over a broad range of interest. His was a revolutionary, a Marxist mind, ever critical and open, aware that new revolutions always present new qualities and new problems. He did not cringe before them, but faced them boldly and sought solutions.

He saw the Latin American revolution as a long, hard struggle on a Continental scale. Of this he was sure: the necessity in Latin America of armed struggle in most cases, that will in "Our America, almost certainly have the characteristic of becoming a Socialist Revolution," as he said in the last article he ever wrote (in May 1967, for *Tricontinental* magazine in Havana).

Beyond the Continent, he saw the entire complex of world relations. Among his many civilian duties in Cuba, he was a prime mover in establishing bonds with other socialist countries, visiting the Soviet Union on special missions three times, and heading delegations to China, and other socialist lands. He saw a community of interest among three small socialist countries, each confronting in its own way the might of U.S. imperialism —Vietnam, Korea and Cuba. After a visit to seven African countries early in 1965, he declared: "I am convinced it is possible to create a common front of struggle against imperialism, colonialism and neo-colonialism"—the germinal idea of the Organization of Solidarity of the Peoples of Africa, Asia and Latin America. In his last article, full of deep concern for Vietnam and the need for anti-imperialist unity, he wrote: "The time has come to settle our discrepancies and place everything we have at the service of the struggle. . . . In our struggling world, all discrepancies regarding tactics and methods of action for the attainment of limited objectives should be analyzed with the respect that the opinions of others deserve." Che's own opinions certainly deserve the respect and consideration he was ready to give others.

Reading this book one almost touches Che, his humanity, his warmth, his love, and feels the clean sweep of his revolutionary spirit. Perhaps it is now easier to see how natural, how in unison with his way of life, was his decision in the Spring of 1965 to leave high post and honor in Cuba for "other lands that claim the recourse of my modest efforts," as he wrote in his farewell letter. It is easier to sense the abandon with which his restless spirit welcomed new challenges and dangers in pursuit of his great ideal. It was Fidel who said, in his speech announcing the tragic death of Che: "If, as a guerrilla, he had his Achilles' heel, it was this excessively aggressive quality, his absolute contempt of danger." And it was Che himself, in his last sentence of his last article, who wrote his own epitaph:

"Wherever death may surprise us, it will be welcome, provided that this, our battle cry, reach some receptive ear, that another hand be extended to take up our weapons and that other men come foreward to intone our funeral dirge with the staccato of machine guns and new cries of battle and victory."

January 1968   JAMES S. ALLEN

Contents

Foreword

For some time I had contemplated writing a history of the Cuban Revolution that would cover its various aspects and phases. Many leaders of our Revolution have also expressed a similar intention, either in private or publicly, but we have many tasks, the years pass, and the memory of the insurrectional struggle grows dim, making it difficult to detail events that have already become part of America's history.

Presented here are a few personal memories of attacks, skirmishes and battles in which I participated. I do not intend that this fragmentary account, based on recollections and a few hastily-written notes, should be considered a full history of the Revolution. On the contrary, I hope the story will be elaborated by many of those who played a role in the struggle.

My own participation in the war was limited to certain areas of Cuba. It is therefore impossible for me to describe events and battles occurring elsewhere. To help our comrades supply their stories in chronological order, I start with our first battle—the surprise attack upon us at Alegría de Pío, the only battle with Fidel's participation in which we were not victorious.

There are many survivors of these actions and each is invited to contribute to the written record of our history his own recollections of the events. We ask that the narrator be truthful and that in an attempt to describe his contribution he does not exaggerate his real role or pretend to have been where he was not. It is suggested that after writing a few pages to the best of his ability he examine his efforts critically and delete every doubtful fact which weakens the authenticity of his account. In this spirit I begin our memoirs.

ERNESTO CHE GUEVARA

1

Alegría de Pío

Alegría de Pío is in Oriente province, municipality of Niquero, near Cabo Cruz. It was at this very spot, on December 5, 1956, that Batista's forces discovered our hiding place.

We were exhausted from a long, painful march—more painful than long, to tell the truth. We had landed on December 2 at Playa de las Coloradas. All our equipment had been lost, and we had trudged for endless hours through marshland and swamp. All of us were wearing new boots and we were now suffering from blisters and sores. But new footwear and fungus were by no means our only enemies.

We had reached Cuba after a seven-day voyage across the Gulf of Mexico and the Caribbean Sea, without food, plagued by seasickness and aboard a vessel far from seaworthy. We had left the port of Tuxpán (Mexico) November 25, with a stiff northerly wind blowing, and all small craft had been warned to remain in port. The experience had left a deep mark upon our troop of rookies who did not know the meaning of combat.

Of our war equipment all that remained were our rifles, cartridge belts and some wet rounds of ammunition. Our medical supplies were gone and most of our knapsacks had been abandoned in the swamps. We had spent the previous night in a canefield of the Niquero sugar mill, then owned by Julio Lobo. We had managed to assuage our hunger and thirst by eating sugar cane but, lacking experience, we had left a trail of cane peelings and bagasse all over the place. Not that the guards searching for us needed a trail to trace our steps—it had been our guide, as we discovered later, who had betrayed us. The night before we had let him go.

This was an error we were to repeat until in our long struggle we learned that civilians whose personal background was unknown to us were not to be trusted while in dangerous areas. To release that man was a serious blunder.

By daybreak of the 5th we could hardly walk. Near collapse, we would walk a short distance and then beg for a long rest period. We were given orders to halt at the edge of a canefield, in a thicket near a dense woods. Throughout the morning hours most of us slept.

At noon we noticed unusual signs of activity. Air Force piper planes and other small military, as well as private, aircraft began to circle over our hiding place. Most of our men continued cutting and eating sugar cane without realizing they were clearly visible from the planes, now slowly circling at low altitude. I was the troop physician and it was my duty to treat the blistered feet. I recall my last patient that morning, Humberto Lamotte. It was to be his last day on earth. I still remember how tired and worn he looked as he walked to his post from my improvised first-aid station, still carrying his shoes in one hand.

Comrade Montané and I were leaning against a tree, eating our meager rations—half a sausage and two crackers —when a rifle shot broke the stillness. Immediately, a hail of bullets—at least this is the way it seemed to us in our first baptism of fire—descended upon our 82-man force. My rifle was not of the best; I had asked for it deliberately because I was in very poor physical condition from an attack of asthma that had plagued me during our ocean voyage and I did not want to be held responsible for the loss of a good weapon.

What happened after the first burst of fire I can barely remember. Almeida approached requesting orders, but nobody was there to issue them. Later I was told that Fidel had attempted vainly to gather everyone together in the adjoining canefield which could be reached simply by crossing a path. The surprise attack and the heavy gunfire had been too much for us. Almeida ran back to take charge of his group. A comrade dropped a box of ammunition at my feet. When I reprimanded him he looked at me with an expression of anguish and muttered something like "this is no time to bother with ammunition boxes." He continued on his way to the canefield and disappeared from view. He was murdered by Batista's henchmen some time later.

Perhaps this was the first time I was faced with the dilemma of choosing between my devotion to medicine and my duty as a revolutionary soldier. There, at my feet, was a knapsack full of medicine and a box of ammunition. I could not possibly carry both; they were too heavy. I picked up the box of ammunition, leaving the medicine, and started to cross the clearing, heading for the canefield.

I remember Faustino Pérez, kneeling and firing his machine-gun pistol. Near me a comrade, Arbentosa, was walking toward the canefield. A burst of fire hit us both. I felt a sharp blow on my chest and a wound in the neck, and I thought for certain I was dead. Arbentosa, vomiting blood and bleeding profusely from a deep hole made by a 45-caliber bullet, shouted, "They have killed me!" and fired his rifle at no one in particular. Flat on the ground, I turned to Faustino and said, "I've been hit!"—what I actually said is unprintable. Still firing away, Faustino looked at me and said, "Oh, it's nothing," but I could see by the look in his eyes that he thought me as good as dead.

Still on the ground, I fired a shot in the direction of the woods, on an impulse similar to the other wounded man's. Immediately, I began to think about the best way to die. I recalled a Jack London story in which the hero, aware that he is certain to freeze to death in the wastes of Alaska, leans calmly against a tree and prepares to die in a dignified manner. That was the only thing that came to mind at that moment. Someone on his knees said we had better surrender and I heard a voice (later I learned it was Camilo Cienfuegos) shouting, "No, nobody surrenders here!"—followed by a four-letter word. Ponce came at a run, breathing hard, to show me a bullet wound—I was sure the bullet must have pierced his lung. He said, "I'm wounded," and I replied coolly, "Me, too." Then Ponce and other comrades, who were still unhurt, crawled toward the canefield.

For a moment I was left alone, lying there waiting to die. Almeida came and urged me to go on. Despite the intense pain I dragged myself into the canefield. There I met comrade Raúl Suárez, whose thumb had been blown off by a rifle bullet; Faustino Pérez was bandaging his hand. Then everything became a blur of airplanes flying low and strafing the field, adding to the confusion, amid Dantesque and grotesque scenes such as the one of a comrade with considerable avoirdupois desperately trying to hide behind a single stalk of sugar cane, while amidst the turmoil someone kept on yelling, "Silence!"

We organized a group headed by Almeida. It included Lieutenant Ramiro Valdés (now a Major) and comrades Chao and Benítez. Almeida leading, we crossed the last path in the rows of cane and reached the safety of the woods. The first shouts of "fire!" were heard from the canefield and tongues of flame and columns of smoke began to rise. I cannot remember exactly what happened. I felt the bitterness of defeat and I was sure I was going to die. We walked until darkness made it impossible to go on, when we decided to go to sleep, huddled together in a heap. We were starved and thirsty and the mosquitoes increased our misery. This was our baptism of fire on December 5, 1956, at the outskirts of Niquero. It was the beginning of what would later become the Rebel Army.

2

Battle of La Plata

Our first victory was a successful attack upon a small army garrison at the mouth of La Plata river. Our victory had an electrifying effect. It was like a clarion call, announcing that the Rebel Army really existed and was ready to fight. For us, it was confirmation of our hopes for total victory.

On January 14, 1957, shortly after the surprise attack upon us at Alegría de Pío, we came to a halt by the Magdalena river. A stretch of solid land, starting at the Sierras, juts out between the Magdalena and La Plata rivers. Fidel ordered target practice as a first attempt at training of a sort for our troop. Some were using a weapon for the first time in their lives. We had not washed for many days and we welcomed the opportunity for a swim. Those who had them changed into clean clothes. Our weapons at that time were: nine rifles equipped with telescopic sights, five semi-automatic rifles, four bolt rifles, two Thompson sub-machine guns and a 16-gauge shotgun.

That afternoon we climbed the last hill before reaching the outskirts of La Plata. We were following a trail marked out for us by a peasant, Melquiades Elías. He had been recommended by our guide, Eutimio Guerra. Our guide was essential to us. He seemed to be the prototype of the rebel farmer, but later he was caught by Casillas [the Major in charge of Batista's troops in the area] who, instead of killing him, bribed him with an offer of $10,000 and the rank of lieutenant if he managed to kill Fidel. Eutimio came close to fulfilling his bargain, but he lacked the courage. Nevertheless, he proved very useful to the enemy because he revealed the location of several of our camps.

At that time Eutimio was serving us loyally. He was one

of many peasants fighting for land, and anyone fighting the landowners also had to fight the guards in their service.

That day we captured two peasants who turned out to be cousins of our guide. We released one but kept the other as a precautionary measure. The next day, January 15, we had a look at the La Plata army barracks, then under con-construction. Some half-naked men were moving about, but we could tell they were soldiers. Just before sundown, about 6 P.M., a boat came in and some guards landed while others went aboard. We could not make out exactly what was happening, so we postponed the attack to the following day.

At dawn of the 16th we again began watching the army post. During the night the boat had gone. No soldiers could be seen anywhere. At 3 P.M. we decided to approach the road leading to the barracks and take a look. By nightfall we crossed the shallow La Plata and took positions on the road. Five minutes later we took two farmers into custody. One had a record as an informer. When we revealed who we were and gave them assurance that no harm would befall them, they gave us some valuable information: there were no more than 15 soldiers in the barracks; also, Chicho Osorio, among the region's most notorious foremen, was due to come by at any moment. He worked for the Laviti family plantation. The Lavitis had established an enormous domain, protecting it by means of a terror regime with the help of characters like Chicho Osorio.

Soon Chicho appeared astride a mule, with a little Negro lad riding "double." Chicho was drunk. Universo Sánchez ordered him to halt in the name of the rural guards, and pronto Chicho replied, "Mosquito." It was the password.

We must have looked like a gang of pirates, but Chicho was so drunk we were able to fool him. Fidel stepped forward; acting very indignant, he said he was an army colonel who had come to investigate why the rebels had not yet been liquidated. He bragged about going into the woods, thus accounting for his beard. He talked of how the army was "botching up things," and so on. In a word, he made mince-meat of army efficiency. Sheepishly, Chicho Osorio admitted the guards spent all their time in the barracks, eating and doing nothing except occasionally going out on useless rounds. He agreed heartily that the rebels must be wiped out. We interrogated him discreetly about "friendly" and "unfriendly" people in the area and we interpreted his replies in reverse: when Osorio labeled someone bad we knew he was one of our friends, and so on. By now we had a couple dozen names and Osorio was still jabbering away. He related how two men had been killed, adding, "But my General Batista set me free at once." He told of slapping two peasants who "had gotten somewhat out of hand," claiming that guards would not do that but would let the peasants talk without punishing them.

Fidel asked what he would do if he ever caught Fidel Castro. Osorio replied, with a very expressive gesture, "We'll have to cut his . . . off." He said the same about Crescencio. "Look," he said, pointing to his shoes, which were the same Mexican type our men wore. "These shoes belonged to one of those sons-of-bitches we killed." Without realizing it, Osorio had signed his own sentence. On Fidel's suggestion, he agreed to accompany us to the barracks to take the soldiers by surprise and thus prove to them how badly prepared and unfit for duty they were.

As we neared the barracks, with Osorio in the lead, I still felt that he might have become wise to our trick. However, in complete ignorance, he kept going on, for he was so drunk he could not think straight. When we crossed the river to approach the barracks Fidel told Osorio that under military rules the prisoner has to be tied up. He did not resist, and went on, this time as a prisoner, although he was unaware of how real it was. He explained that guards were posted only at the entrance to the barracks under construction and at the house of a foreman named Honorio. Osorio guided us to a place near the barracks, close by the road to Macío. Luis Crespo (now a Major) went ahead to scout around and returned to confirm Osorio's report. Crespo had seen the barracks and the pinpoints of light from the guards' cigarettes.

As we were about to approach the barracks we had to pull back into the woods to let three guards on horseback pass. In front of them walked a prisoner whom they were urging to go faster, hurling all sorts of insults at him. They passed very close to me and I recall the peasant pleading, "I'm just like you fellows," and the reply from one whom we later learned was Corporal Basol: "Shut up, and get going or I'll use the whip on you!" We thought the peasant was out of danger, since at the moment of the attack he was not in the barracks. However, the following day when the guards heard of the attack they murdered him in Macío.

We had 22 weapons. It was a crucial moment because we were short of ammunition. The army post had to be taken, since failure would have meant spending all our ammunition, leaving us practically defenseless. Lieutenant Julito Díaz (later killed at the battle of El Uvero), Camilo Cienfuegos, Benítez and Calixto Morales, armed with semi-automatic rifles, were to surround the palm-thatched house on the right. Fidel, Universo Sánchez, Luis Crespo, Calixto García, Fajardo (brother of our physician, Piti Fajardo, killed in the Escambray) and myself would attack the center. Raúl and his squad and Almeida with his would attack the barracks from the right flank.

We approached to within 40 yards of the barracks. By the light of a full moon, Fidel opened hostilities with two bursts of machine-gun fire and all available rifles joined in. At once, we demanded the enemy's surrender, but with no results. Murderer-informer Osorio was executed as soon as the battle began.

The attack started at 2:40 A.M. and the guards put up a much stiffer resistance than we had expected. Every time we asked them to surrender, a sergeant opened up with a burst from his M-1. Orders were given to use our old, Brazilian-type hand grenades. Luis Crespo and I threw ours, but they did not go off. Raúl Castro threw a stick of dynamite which also failed to explode. It was now necessary to get close to the buildings and set them afire, even at the risks of our lives. Universo Sánchez made a futile attempt and Cienfuegos also failed. Finally, Luis Crespo and I got close to one of the sheds and set it on fire. The glare revealed that it was a place for storing coconuts, but the soldiers were intimidated and they gave up the fight. One, trying to escape, ran smack into Luis Crespo's rifle. Crespo shot him in the chest, took the soldier's rifle and continued firing toward the house. Entrenched behind a tree, Camilo Cienfuegos shot at the fleeing sergeant but ran out of ammunition.

Almost defenseless, the soldiers were being wiped out by our bullets. Camilo was the first into the house, and shouts of surrender were heard. Quickly we took stock of our booty: eight Springfields, one Thompson machine gun and about 1,000 rounds. We had fired approximately 500 rounds. We also took cartridge belts, fuel, knives, clothing and some food. Casualties: two soldiers dead, five wounded. We took three prisoners.

Not a single scratch was suffered by our men. We set fire to the soldiers' quarters and we withdrew after taking care of the wounded (three were in serious condition and we learned later that they died). One of the soldiers later joined the forces under Major Raúl Castro, was promoted to lieutenant, and died in an airplane accident after the war.

Our attitude to the wounded was in sharp contrast to the enemy's. They not only killed our wounded but they abandoned their own. This difference greatly impressed the enemy forces and it was instrumental in our victory. Fidel ordered that all our medicine be given the prisoners to take care of the wounded. I was appalled; as a physician, I felt the need to save all avaliable medicine and drugs for our own men. We freed all civilians and at 4.30 A.M. of the 17th we started for Palma Mocha, arriving at dawn and continuing toward the most inaccessible zones of the Sierra Maestra.

A most depressing scene awaited us. The day before, an army corporal and a foreman had warned all families in the area that the Air Force was to bomb the entire zone, and the exodus toward the coast had begun. Since no one knew of our presence in the area, it was obviously a trick by the foreman and the rural guards to take the land away from the peasants. Unfortunately, their stories had co-incided with our attack, giving their lie an appearance of truth. Terror was rampant among the peasants and it was impossible for us to stop their flight.

This was the first victorious battle of the rebel forces. Only in this battle and the following one did we have more weapons than men. Peasants were not yet ready to join the struggle, and communications with the city bases practically did not exist.

3

Battle of Arroyo del Infierno

Arroyo del Infierno is a small stream running into the Palma Mocha river. Walking along the stream, skirting the surrounding hills in a direction away from the river, we came upon a small gorge with two palm-thatched huts. We set up camp, as usual keeping away from the huts.

Fidel expected the army would come looking for us with more or less success, so he decided to set up an ambush to capture a few soldiers. Accordingly, men were posted at appropriate spots. Fidel kept a constant check on our lines and defenses. On January 19, while we were reviewing the troops, an accident occurred that could have led to grave consequences. At that time I wore a corporal's helmet, a trophy of the La Plata battle. As I reviewed the troops I wore the helmet proudly. The review was held in the midst of the woods. Our advance guard heard us coming and they saw a group led by a man with a helmet. Fortunately, it was weapon-cleaning time and Camilo's rifle was the only weapon at hand. He opened fire on us but almost immediately realized his mistake; luckily, the first shot missed and then his automatic rifle jammed. The incident reveals how tense we were, waiting for the fight as a sort of relief from tension. In times such as these, even the coolest of men feel a slight tremor in their legs as everyone anxiously awaits that great moment of war: combat. To be sure, we were far from yearning for a fight. We fought because we had to.

At dawn of the 22nd we heard shots near the Palma Mocha area. This compelled us to strengthen our lines anew and to take up positions to await the enemy troops.

Expecting the soldiers to be nearby, we skipped breakfast and lunch. Crespo and some others had discovered a hen's nest, and we stole the eggs, taking care to leave one so as not to discourage the hen in her task. That morning Crespo decided that since we had heard shots close by we might as well eat the last egg.

At noon we heard somebody in one of the huts. At first we thought it was one of our comrades who had disobeyed orders to stay away. It turned out that it was a soldier. Later the number of soldiers grew to six. Finally, some left. We could see the soldier on guard taking a good look around. Then he picked up a few leaves and placed them behind his ears in a sorry attempt at camouflage. Through the telescopic lens he could clearly be seen as he sat in the shade with a placid look on his face. Fidel opened fire, hitting the soldier who fell, crying out what sounded like, "Oh, mother!" and then lay still. Shooting became general and two more soldiers fell. I then saw another soldier trying to hide behind the other hut. From an elevated point all I could see were his legs, the overhanging roof hiding the rest of him. My first shot missed but the second hit. As he fell his rifle hit the ground bayonet first and remained stuck there. Covered by Crespo, I reached the hut and found the man was dead. I took his ammunition, rifle and other belongings. He must have died instantly because rigor mortis was setting in quickly, probably due to exhaustion after his long march through the woods.

It was a fast and furious battle, and soon we were on our way into hiding, having accomplished our task.

When we took inventory it turned out that we had spent about 900 rounds and taken in only 70 from a cartridge belt and one rifle. It was a Garand that went to Efigenio Ameijeiras (now a Major) who used it during most of the war. We counted four enemy dead, but months later we learned from an informer that there had been five. It was not a complete victory but neither was it a Pyrrhic one. We had exchanged blows with the enemy under difficult circumstances and we had passed the test.

Our spirits were raised, helping us to keep climbing toward the most inaccessible spots to escape larger groups of enemy soldiers. We crossed the mountains and now we were traveling parallel to the Batista forces who had also run away, crossing the same mountain tops to get to the other side. For two days our troops and theirs marched almost side by side, quite unaware of each other. Once they spent the night in a hut separated from the hut we occupied only by a narrow river and a couple of road bends. The soldiers were led by Lieutenant Sánchez Mosquera. His name and his fierce reputation were well known all over the Sierra. It is worth recording that the shots we had heard prior to the battle had killed a man of Haitian descent who had refused to guide the soldiers to our hiding place. If the soldiers had not murdered him they would have found us less prepared for battle.

Now again we were overburdened; most were carrying two rifles each. It did not make our traveling easier, but our morale was quite different than after the Alegría de Pío disaster. Only a few days ago we had defeated a smaller

number of men entrenched in an army post; now we had
defeated a column on the march, of greater strength than
ours, and we were able to verify how important it is in this
type of war to eliminate the advance guard, because an
army cannot move without an advance guard.

4

Air Attack

Following our victorious battle against Sánchez Mosquera's men we traveled along the banks of La Plata river.
Then we crossed the Magdalena and returned to Caracas,
a zone familiar to us. But conditions there were much
different than the first time we had hidden on that very
same hill. At that time, everyone in the area supported
our struggle; now Casillas' troops had passed by, leaving
a trail of terror. The peasants had disappeared and there
remained only their huts and a few animals, which we had
to kill for food. Experience had shown us that it was not
safe to stay in the houses, so after we spent one night in one
of these lonely huts we returned to the woods and set up
camp near a waterfall, almost at the top of Caracas hill.

There I received a note from Manuel Fajardo, asking if it
were true that we might possibly lose the war. Our reply,
independent of the state of euphoria following a victory, was
always the same: the war would be won. Fajardo explained
that he asked the question because "Gallego" Morán had
told him it was impossible to win, that our cause was lost.
Morán had ended by urging Fajardo to give up the struggle.
I reported to Fidel, and I discovered that Morán had taken
care to tell Fidel in advance that he was going to put out a
few "feelers" to test the troops' morale. Fidel and I agreed
that this was not the best way, and Fidel addressed the
troops urging a stricter discipline and explaining the perils

involved if discipline was not observed. He also announced that the crimes of insubordination, desertion and defeatism were to be punished by death.

The situation was not a happy one. Our column lacked cohesion. It had neither the ideological awareness nor the *esprit de corps* that can be attained only through hard, bitter struggle. Day after day, more comrades would ask to be released and to be assigned to missions in the cities—although this involved even greater danger—but it was evident that they simply could not stand the rough going. Nevertheless, we maintained our daily routine. Morán went here and there, trying to locate some food and making contacts with neighboring peasants.

This was the general state of affairs on the morning of January 30. Eutimio Guerra, the traitor, had asked Fidel's permission to visit his sick mother; Fidel had agreed, and gave him money for the trip which Eutimio had said would take several weeks. (We were still unaware of many strange things which later became quite clear due to Eutimio's behavior following his return.) He had told us that he was near Palma Mocha when he discovered that the army was hard on our trail, and had tried to warn us but all he found were the bodies of dead soldiers in the house of Delfín, a peasant who lived near Arroyo del Infierno, where the battle had taken place; he had followed our vague trail until he found our camp. What actually happened was that Eutimio had been captured by the army and now he was working as an enemy agent. He had been promised a large sum of money and a military rank as a reward for murdering Fidel.

As part of his plan, Eutimio left the camp on the night of the 29th. In the early hours of January 30 we heard the sound of airplane engines. Our field kitchen was set up 200 yards downhill, near a brook. Suddenly, we heard a plane diving and the rattle of machine guns, followed by falling bombs. We still lacked experience and it seemed to us that the gunfire came from every side. Fifty-caliber shells explode on contact with the ground, and we thus got the impression that shooting came from the woods, in addition to the air strafing. We thought we were surrounded by the enemy.

I was assigned the mission to wait for the members of the advance guard and pick up a few utensils we had abandoned following the attack. The meeting point was to be La Cueva del Humo. Accompanied by Chao, a Spanish War veteran, I waited for our men but they did not show up. Carrying a heavy load, we followed a trail and finally sat down to rest. Then we heard sounds and saw Guillermo García (now a Major) and Sergio Acuña coming down the same trail we had followed. They were from the advance guard. After a brief consultation, García and I returned to the camp to be met by a scene of desolation. Everything was silent now, and the planes were gone. In a unique display of marksmanship, never again equaled throughout the entire war, the Air Force had hit our field kitchen smack on the nose. The stove was cut in half. A bomb had hit our advance post, but luckily the men had already abandoned it. Morán, who had gone scouting with another man, returned alone, saying that he had seen five planes and that there were no soldiers in the vicinity. All five of us started out, carrying our heavy loads. Suddenly, we came upon a scene of horror; our peasant friend's house was burned to the ground. All that remained were a cat, meowing sadly, and a pig that took off into the woods as soon as he saw us. We had heard about La Cueva del Humo but were not sure about its location. We spent a sleepless night, waiting for our comrades and fearing an encounter with the enemy.

On January 31, we camped atop a hill overlooking some orchards. We explored an area we believed to be La Cueva del Humo but found nothing. Sergio thought he had seen some men wearing baseball caps, but he was late reporting to us and we could not see anyone. We went with Guillermo to explore the bottom of the valley near the Ají. A friend of

Guillermo's gave us some food, but everybody in the area was scared to death. This man said that Ciro Frías' merchandise had been seized and burned by the guards, his mules impounded and the muleteer killed. The soldiers, who had arrived that morning, were under the command of Major Casillas, who had spent the night near the house.

On February 1, we were still in our camp, in the open. At 11 A.M. we heard shots and someone calling for help. This was too much for Sergio Acuña, who dropped his rifle and cartridge belt and disappeared silently into the woods, deserting his post. In our campaign diary we entered a list of items he had taken with him: a can of condensed milk and three sausages. We were very sorry about the milk and sausages. A few hours later, we heard noises, and not knowing whether Sergio had betrayed us, we prepared to defend ourselves. It turned out to be Crescencio, leading a large troop, including some of our men and a group from Manzanillo, led by Roberto Pesant. Missing from our group were: Sergio Acuña, the deserter; Calixto Morales, Calixto García, Manuel Acuña, and a new recruit who apparently got lost during the shooting.

Once again we started toward the valley and on the way down we distributed the items the men from Manzanillo had brought. These included a surgery kit for me and a change of clothes for everyone. We were moved by the initials that the girls from Manzanillo had embroidered on our uniforms.

The following day, February 2, two months after the *Granma* landing, we were a stronger group; we had ten more men from Manzanillo and we felt stronger and more confident than ever before. We held long discussions about the surprise air attack and we all agreed that the smoke from the open field kitchen had served as a beacon for the planes. For many months—perhaps for the duration of the war—the memory of that surprise attack remained with us and open-air cooking was avoided for fear of unpleasant consequences.

At that time, we would have found it impossible to believe that Eutimio Guerra, the traitor, had been a passenger in the observation plane carrying Casillas, and had pointed out our hiding place. The story about his mother's illness had been a pretext to go out and find Casillas to tell him where we were.

For a long time Eutimio Guerra played an important negative role in the development of our war of liberation.

5

Surprise Attack at Altos de Espinosa

Following the surprise attack mentioned in the previous chapter, we left Caracas hill in search for more familiar ground where we could establish direct contact with Manzanillo, receive additional aid, and obtain information on the situation in the rest of the country.

We therefore returned to the Ají, traveling over familiar territory, until we reached old Mendoza's house. On the hillsides we had to cut our way through the brush with our machetes, and progress was difficult. We spent the night on a hill, with practically nothing to eat. I still remember one of the greatest banquets I ever attended: Crespo showed up with a can of four sausages which he had "saved" for his friends. Crespo, Fidel and I, together with others, ate the meager ration with great joy. Our journey continued until we reached the house "to the right of Caracas hill," where old Mendoza was to give us food. In spite of his fright, this loyal peasant would welcome us every time we passed, encouraged by Crescencio or some other friendly peasants who were now part of our troop.

It was a painful journey for me. I was suffering from an attack of malaria; both Crespo and the unforgettable Julio Zenón Acosta nursed me throughout the entire trip. It was not our habit to spend the night indoors, but my condition and that of Morán, who was always finding an excuse to get sick, made it necessary for us to sleep in one of the houses, while the rest of the men kept watch outside. They used the house only for eating.

It was necessary to "clean up" our group. A few men were of very low morale and others were seriously hurt, among them Ramiro Valdés (now Minister of the Interior) and Ignacio Pérez, one of Crescencio's sons later killed in action holding the rank of captain. Ramiro had received a blow on a knee already weakened by wounds received in the Moncada attack,[1] so we had to leave him. Several men left but we considered their defection very advantageous to our troop. I remember one of them who had a nervous breakdown and suddenly, in the stillness of the woods, began to shout that he had been sent to a camp with plenty of food and water and an anti-aircraft defense, and now he was being chased by planes and there was no place to hide, no food, and no water. A similar condition is common to most men during the first few days of war. Later, those who stay and pass the first tests become accustomed to the filth, the want of water and food and the lack of safety, placing all their trust in their rifles as well as in the cohesion and resistance of the small guerrilla group.

Ciro Frías arrived, accompanied by a few new men. He told us some stories that caused considerable confusion. Now we smile when we think of it, but at that time it was no joke. He had been told that Díaz Tamayo[2] was about to make an about-face and was "dealing" with the revolutionary forces; that Faustino had been able to collect thousands of dollars; in one word, that sabotage was rampant and the end of the government was drawing near. There was also a sad note, but it served as a warning: Sergio Acuña, the deserter, had gone to some relative's house; there he bragged about his heroic deeds in the Sierra and was heard by one, Pedro Herrera, who informed the police. The notorious Corporal Roselló (later executed by the people) arrested Acuña, tortured him, fired four shots into him and hung him. It was a great lesson for our troop; it showed the value of cohesion and the futility of trying to escape from a danger that threatened every one of us. It also made it imperative for us to move to another location; possibly the boy might have talked before he was murdered, and he knew Florentino's house, where we were at the moment.

A curious incident occurred which we did not quite understand until some time later. Eutimio Guerra had told us that he had dreamed about Acuña's death. He even added that Corporal Roselló had been the killer. This led to a long philosophical discussion on whether or not it was possible to predict an event from dreams. Part of my daily routine was to lecture the men on a cultural or political subject. I explained that such a thing was not possible; that it was due to an extraordinary coincidence; that we all expected Acuña to end that way, and that we all knew that Roselló was running wild all over that zone. Universo Sánchez settled the whole affair by saying that Eutimio had the habit of telling tall tales and that someone had probably told him the entire story; we must remember that Eutimio had left the day before and had returned with 50 cans of milk and a flashlight.

One of the staunchest supporters of the theory of "illumination" was the 45-year-old peasant, Julio Zenón Acosta. He was my first pupil in the Sierra. I was doing my best to teach him to read and write and wherever we stopped we'd take up the lessons. We had reached the stage of distinguishing A from O, E from I, and so on. Julio Zenón, not thinking of the years past but rather of the years to come, had put his heart into learning how to read and write. Perhaps he could be a very good example to peasants who were his comrades at that time, or to others who might hear about him. Julio Zenón Acosta was of great help to us in those difficult times. He never tired, he knew the zone well, and he was the first to run to the aid of a comrade in trouble, or help a city man who was still unfamiliar with his surroundings. He would bring water from a distant stream, start a fire and find the right kind of kindling to get it going on a rainy day. He was our all-round man.

One night, only a short time before we discovered he was a traitor, Eutimio complained that he had no blanket and asked Fidel to lend him one. It was a cold February night, up in the hills. Fidel replied that if he gave Eutimio his blanket they would both be cold; it was better to share the blanket, topped by two of Fidel's coats. That night, Eutimio Guerra, armed with a 45-caliber pistol that Casillas had given him to use against Fidel and with two hand grenades that were to be used to cover his getaway once the crime had been committed, slept side by side with our leader. Universo Sánchez and I had made it a point to stay close to Fidel and that night Eutimio had said to us: "I am very interested in this business of the watch. We must be on guard at all times." We explained that three men were on guard nearby. We, the *Granma* veterans, and a few of Fidel's trusted men always took turns protecting him. Thus, Eutimio spent an entire night lying side by side with the leader of the Revolution, waiting for the chance to murder him, but he never gathered enough courage. Throughout the night, the fate of the Revolution to a large extent depended on the conflicts between courage and fear, scruples and ambition for power and money, running through the mind of a traitor. Fortunately for us, the sum total of inhibitory factors emerged triumphant and the night passed without any incident.

We had left Florentino's house and were now settled in a ravine. Ciro Frías had gone home and returned with a few hens and some other food. Hot soup and other viands were our reward for a long, rainy night in the open. Somebody said Eutimio had been around there too. Eutimio used to go in and out at will; we trusted him and we had accepted his explanation of his trip to see his sick mother, the story about the Caracas hill battle, and so on. He said his mother had recovered from her illness. The man was extremely audacious. We were in a place called Altos de Espinosa, near a chain of hills—El Lomón, Loma del Burro, Caracas, and others—under constant aerial attack. Eutimio would say: "I told you they'd strafe Loma del Burro today." The planes would come and strafe the hill and Eutimio would jump to his feet, bragging about his accurate forecasting.

On February 9, 1957, Ciro Frías and Luis Crespo went foraging for food as usual. Everything was quiet, and about 10 A.M. a young peasant named Labrada, who had recently joined our group, captured a man nearby. He turned out to be one of Crescencio's relatives, a sales-clerk in Celestino's grocery store where Casillas' soldiers were stationed. The boy reported that close to 145 soldiers were at the house. We checked, and we saw a few, far away on a barren spot. Our prisoner told us that he had spoken to Eutimio, who had told him that the zone was to be bombed the next day. Casillas' men moved about but we could not determine which way. Fidel became suspicious; Eutimio's strange behavior was beginning to dawn upon us and we began to comment on it. At 1:30 P.M. Fidel gave orders to leave and we went to the top of the hill to wait for the comrades who had gone scouting. Ciro Frías and Luis Crespo returned, saying that everything was normal.

Suddenly Frías requested silence saying that he saw someone moving around. He cocked his rifle and at that moment we heard a shot, followed by a volley. The sound of volleys and explosions came from the place we had just occupied and which was now being torn apart by concentrated fire. We left our position at full speed and some time later we learned that Julio Zenón Acosta had been killed atop the hill. The uneducated peasant, who was able to comprehend the enormous tasks that the Revolution would face following its triumph, the man who was getting ready to lend a hand in these tasks, was dead. Our group dispersed. My knapsack, my pride and joy, full of medicine, reserve food, a few books and blankets, was left behind. I managed to pull out a blanket that had belonged to Batista's army, a trophy of the La Plata battle, and started to run.

Soon I met a small group: Almeida, Julito Díaz, Universo Sánchez, Camilo Cienfuegos, Guillermo García, Ciro Frías, Motolá, Pesant, Emilio Labrada and Yayo. We took off in an oblique direction, trying to avoid the shots. We did not know where our comrades were or what had happened to them. We could hear shots in our rear, and we knew our trail was easy to follow because we were moving fast and did not have time to erase our tracks. At 5:15 P.M. we reached a craggy spot, where the woods ended. We made up our minds to wait there until darkness because if we tried to cross the open space by daylight, the enemy would see us. If they followed us to our present location, we could still defend ourselves, protected by the rugged terrain. However, the enemy did not show up and we went on, guided by Ciro Frías, who was slightly familiar with the area. It had been suggested that the group be broken into two patrols, allowing for faster movement and less conspicious trail, but Almeida and I voted against the idea. We wanted to keep the group intact. We reconnoitered the area, known as Limones, and held a meeting because some of the men wanted to get away from there. Almeida, head of the group, based on his rank of Captain, gave orders to continue to El Lomón, which Fidel had fixed for the meeting place. Some of the men argued that the place was familiar to Eutimio and we would find the soldiers there. We now had no doubts about Eutimio being a traitor, but it was Almeida's decision to obey Fidel's orders.

We met Fidel on February 12 near El Lomón in a place called Derecha de la Caridad. Then we heard the whole story about Eutimio. It began with his capture by Casillas following the La Plata encounter. Instead of killing Eutimio, Casillas had bribed him to kill Fidel. Eutimio had given away our position in Caracas; he had given the order to bomb Loma del Burro because it was on our itinerary—we had changed it at the last moment—and he had organized the concentrated attack at Cañón del Arroyo from where we withdrew with only one casualty thanks to Fidel's quick thinking. We verified the death of Julio Acosta and it was said that some guards had been killed and others wounded. I must confess that neither the dead nor the wounded was any of my own doing; at the time, I had executed a "strategic retreat" at full speed.

Now we were all together, except one comrade lost the day before. Raúl, Ameijeiras, Ciro Redondo, Manuel Fajardo, Echeverría, Morán, and Fidel; in all, 18 of us. This was the "Re-unified Revolutionary Army" on February 12, 1957. A few comrades had already given up and a few rookies gave up their guerrilla war right then and there. A *Granma* veteran was also missing. His name was Armando Rodríguez and he carried a Thompson machine gun. For the last few days he had looked so alarmed and frightened every time we heard shots around us, particularly if the shots came from all sides, that we began to describe his expression as a "surrounding maneuver look." Every time a man's face showed the look of a trapped animal we expected something unpleasant to happen. That type of look was incompatible with guerrilla warfare. Our friend with the "surrounding maneuver look" got into high gear, as we used to say in guerrilla jargon, and took off. Some time later, we found his machine gun abandoned in a peasant's hut, a great distance away. Undoubtedly, the man was gifted with a good pair of legs!

6

End of a Traitor

Once our little army was organized, we decided to abandon the El Lomón region. On the way, we made contact with peasants and established bases necessary for our survival. We kept going away from the Sierra Maestra, toward the plains where we could get in touch with the comrades operating in the cities.

We passed by the hamlet of La Montería and camped in a thicket of woods near a stream, on a plantation owned by Epifanio Díaz, whose sons had joined the Revolution.

We wanted closer contact with the 26th of July Movement. Our nomad existence made it practically impossible to contact its members.

Actually, we were two distinct groups having different tactics and strategy. The great split[3] that months later was to imperil the Movement's unity had not yet materialized, but one already could feel that the concepts were different.

It was on this farm that we met the outstanding figures of the Movement in the city, among them three women, today well known to all Cuba: Vilma Espín, now President of the Federation of Cuban Women and Raúl Castro's wife; Haydée Santamaría, now President of the Casa de las Américas and Armando Hart's wife, and Celia Sánchez, our beloved comrade in every moment of the struggle, who was soon to join our group for the duration of the war. There was also Faustino Pérez, an old friend and *Granma* comrade, who had come to report to us on his mission to the city and rush back once again. Shortly afterward he was taken prisoner.

We met Armando Hart, and I then had my only opportunity to spend some time with Frank País, the great leader from Santiago.

Frank was one of those men who make a lasting impression at first sight. His present photos are quite accurate but it was his eyes that impressed me most. It is very difficult to write about a comrade now dead, whom I only saw once and whose life is well known to everyone. I could see in his eyes the fire of a man possessed by a cause, with faith in it. It was evident that he was an extraordinary person. Today he is called "the unforgettable Frank País," and that is the way I feel about him, although I only saw him once. Frank is another comrade whose life now would be devoted to the common task of the Socialist Revolution; his loss is part of the enormous price that our people had to pay for their freedom.

He gave us a silent lesson in order and discipline, cleaning our dirty rifles, taking stock of the ammunition and keeping every round in place. Since that first day, I made a pledge to take care of my weapon. I kept my pledge, too, although I must say I was never too meticulous.

The little thicket of woods was the scene of other interesting events. For the first time we were to be interviewed by a reporter, and a foreign reporter at that. This man was Herbert Matthews[4] who brought with him a small box-type camera with which he took pictures that were widely disseminated and later disputed in the stupid statements of one of Batista's ministers. The interpreter was Javier Pazos, who later joined the guerrillas with whom he remained for a long time.

I was not present at the interview. Fidel told me later that Matthews had asked concrete questions. He had posed no "loaded" questions and seemed to sympathize with the Revolution. I remember Fidel telling how he had given an affirmative reply to Matthews' question as to whether Fidel was an anti-imperialist. Fidel had objected to the delivery of armaments to Batista and had told Matthews that the arms were not for intercontinental defense but were to be used against the people.

Matthews' visit was short. Once he left, we got ready to depart. We were warned to keep our eyes open because Eutimio was somewhere nearby. Almeida was ordered to go and capture him. Accompanying him were Julito Díaz, Ciro Frías, Camilo Cienfuegos and Efigenio Ameijeiras. Ciro Frías overpowered Eutimio—not a difficult task—and brought him to us. He was carrying a 45-caliber pistol, three hand grenades and a pass signed by Casillas. By then, Eutimio knew that he was to be executed. He fell to his knees at Fidel's feet and asked simply to be shot, saying that he deserved to die. He seemed to have aged all of a sudden; his temples were gray, something I had never noticed before. There was a tense moment. Fidel began to berate Eutimio, and Eutimio kept asking to be shot. We will never forget the moment when Ciro Frías, who was a close friend of Eutimio's, began to talk to him. He spoke of all the favors he had done for him, of how he and his brother had always helped Eutimio's family. Then he confronted him with his crimes: first, Eutimio had informed on Ciro's brother and the boy had been murdered; next, Eutimio had tried to have our entired group exterminated. It was a long, tragic statement that Eutimio heard without uttering a word. He was asked if he had something to say and he said he wanted the Revolution—that is, us—to take care of his children.

The Revolution kept its promise. Eutimio Guerra is simply a name that comes to mind when writing these notes but otherwise it has been forgotten, perhaps even by his own children. Under a different name, they are now attending school, receiving the same treatment as all other sons of the people, preparing themselves for a better life, but some day they will have to be told that the peasant who let himself be tempted by power and money, although recognizing his crime, never asked for clemency—which he knew he did not deserve—but, instead, asked our leader to be kind and benevolent to his children.

At that moment, a tremendous storm broke out and it grew dark: amidst a veritable deluge interrupted by lightning bolts and thunder, the life of Eutimio Guerra was snuffed out. No one heard the shot that killed him.

We buried him the following day. A little incident occurred when Manuel Fajardo tried to place a cross over the grave. I objected, saying that it would involve great danger for the owner of the farm. Then Fajardo carved a cross on a nearby tree. That is the only sign showing the resting place of a traitor.

Morán quit at that time. He knew we did not care for him and that we all thought of him as a potential deserter.

Recently, he had disappeared for a few days with the excuse that he had been trailing Eutimio and had become lost in the woods.

Just when we were ready to depart, we heard a shot and found Morán with a bullet in his leg. Comrades who happened to be near him held long arguments among themselves. Some said the shot was an accident, while others claimed that Morán had done it on purpose to avoid staying with our group.

Morán's later behavior—his act of treason and his death at the hands of the Guantánamo revolutionaries—make it quite evident that he shot himself intentionally.

Finally, we left the farm. Frank País had promised to send us a group of men around the beginning of March; the rendezvous was to be at Epifanio Díaz' house, near El Jíbaro.

7

Bitter Days

The days following our departure from Epifanio's farm were, at least for me, the most painful of the war. These notes are an attempt to describe the effect upon our men of the initial stage of the revolutionary struggle. If this passage contains more references than the others to myself it is only because it is related to other episodes, and to leave them out would mean a loss of continuity.

Our revolutionary troop was made up of 17 men of the original group and three new recruits: Gil, Sotolongo and Raúl Díaz. These men had arrived in the *Granma,* had hidden away somewhere near Manzanillo, and when they heard of our whereabouts they decided to join us and share our fate. It was very difficult for us at the time to increase our army. Some men came, but others would leave. The struggle demanded a tough physical condition and a high level of morale, living as we did under the threat of continuous attack.

We traveled without a fixed destination, hiding in small wooded areas in a zone where cattle had cleared most of the vegetation. One night we heard on Fidel's little radio that one of the men who had left with Crescencio had been captured. Eutimio had already told us that the man had been arrested but we had never found out for certain. Now at least we knew he was alive. It was not always that a man survived a Batista army "interrogation." Frequently we heard rifle and machine-gun fire directed toward the wooded areas. The soldiers spent a lot of ammunition but never dared enter the woods.

On February 22 I wrote in my diary that I was beginning to feel the symptoms of an attack of asthma; I did not have any anti-asthmatic medicine left. The date for the new rendezvous was set for March 5, so we still had to wait several days.

During that period we moved about aimlessly, killing time and waiting for Frank País' men who were to bring additional weapons. It had been decided that our group was to be strengthened in firepower rather than in numbers, and that every available weapon in Santiago was to be brought to the Sierra Maestra.

Once we spent a very uneasy day by a stream near La Majagua where there was practically no vegetation. It was in a valley named Las Mercedes. It is very hard to remember exact names now. At dusk, we reached the house of a peasant, Emiliano. He was another of those peasants who became frightened every time they met us and yet they risked their lives for us and contributed to the development of the Revolution. It was the rainy season in the Sierra and night after night we would get soaked to the bone, so we now headed for the peasant huts, despite the danger of meeting the soldiers who were everywhere.

My asthma was so bad I could hardly walk, and we spent another night near a house, among a thicket of coffee trees. It was February 27 or 28. Censorship had been discontinued and the radio was pouring out news about everything that had occurred during the last few months.

There was talk about terrorist attacks and about Matthews' interview with Fidel. That was the moment when the Minister of Defense made his famous statement that Matthews' interview was a lie, and demanded that the photographs be published. Hermes, the son of old Emiliano, at the time was the one who would forage and show us the way. On the morning of the 28th he did not make his usual rounds, and Fidel issued immediate orders to move to another place overlooking the roads. About 4 P.M. Universo Sánchez and Luis Crespo, who were watching the road, saw a large troop coming from the direction of Las Vegas. We had to move fast to reach the hillside, and cross over to the other side before the troops cut us off. It was not difficult because we had seen them in time. Mortar and machine-gun fire broke out, headed in our direction, which proved that Batista's men knew that we were somewhere in the vicinity. Everybody made it to the top, but for me it was a terrible experience. I was practically choking by the time I reached the hilltop. I remember Crespo's efforts to make me walk. Every time I said I could go no further and asked to be left behind, Crespo would revert to our jargon and snap at me: "You son-of-a-bitch from Argentina, either you walk or I'll hit you with my rifle butt!" Then he would pick up his load and practically carry me and my heavy knapsack to the top. All this under a heavy downpour.

We reached a small hut at a place called Purgatorio. Fidel put on a great performance, impersonating a "Major González" of Batista's army in search of rebels. The host was both courteous and cool, but another man, a neighbor, was a real toady. I was too ill fully to enjoy the dialogue between Fidel, in his role as Major González, and the man who insisted on giving advice to Fidel and kept saying that he could not understand why this boy Castro was out there fighting in the woods.

Something had to be done about me; I simply could not go on any longer. When the chatty neighbor left, Fidel told the host who he really was and the man threw his arms around him, saying he belonged to the Orthodox party, that he was a follower of Chibás,[5] and that he was ready to help out in every way. It was necessary for the peasant to go to Manzanillo and establish some contact or, at least, buy some medicine. Even his wife was not to know that I would be near the house. Our latest recruit, a man of doubtful reputation, was assigned as my guard. In a generous gesture, Fidel gave me a Johnson rifle, a real jewel. Then we all made a big show of leaving together and a few yards away my companion, whom we called "the teacher," and I went into the woods to hide and wait. The latest news was that Matthews had telephoned to say the photographs were to be published, while Díaz Tamayo insisted that the whole thing was a lie and that nobody could get past the troops surrounding the rebels. Armando Hart was in prison, charged with being the second leader of the Movement. The date was February 28.

Our man fulfilled his mission and I got my adrenalin. The next ten days were the most bitter days of the struggle in the Sierra. I was dragging myself from tree to tree, using my rifle as a crutch, accompanied by a thoroughly frightened man who went practically out of his mind every time I coughed, he was so afraid someone would hear me. But we finally made it back to Epifanio's house. It had taken us ten days to cover a distance easily covered in one day's march. We did not make it in time for the rendezvous scheduled for March 5. Our slow movements and the circle of soldiers surrounding the zone kept us from reaching the house until March 11.

Several things had happened, already known to the members of the household. In a place called Altos de

Meriño, Fidel's group had become separated under the mistaken impression that they were soon to be attacked. Twelve men had followed Fidel and six had gone with Ciro Frías. Ciro's group fell into an ambush but, luckily, they all escaped. Now they were all back. One of them, Yayo, who returned minus his rifle, had stopped by Epifanio's house on his way to Manzanillo and told the whole story. Frank País' troop was ready, although Frank had been arrested. We spoke with the leader of the troop, Captain Jorge Sotús. He told us it was impossible to make the rendezvous by March 5 because the news about their coming had leaked out and the roads were infested with soldiers. We took every measure to insure the arrival of the troop, estimated to be close to 50 men.

8

Reinforcements

On March 13, while we waited for the reinforcements, we heard the news of the attempt to kill Batista. We learned the names of some of the dead: first, José Antonio Echeverría, student leader; then the others, among them, Menelao Mora. Innocent persons were killed, too. The following day we heard that Pelayo Cuervo, an Orthodox party leader who had always maintained a firm position against Batista, had been murdered. His body was found in a desolate spot of the aristocratic residential section of the country club known as "The Little Lake." A strange paradox: Pelayo Cuervo's sons and their father's murderers participated in the thwarted invasion of Playa Girón.[6] They had come to "liberate Cuba from Communist oppression."

A few details filtered through the curtain of censorship surrounding the frustrated attack on the Presidential Palace. I had never met Echeverría, the student leader, but I had

met a few of the others in Mexico during a meeting of the
26th of July Movement and the Students' Directorate[7]
aimed at taking steps toward common action. These men
were: Faure Chomón, who became Cuban Ambassador to
the USSR; Fructuoso Rodríguez and Joe Westbrook. All
three had participated in the attack.

As everyone knows, the attack was thwarted before the
men could reach the third floor of the Palace, where Batista
was. What could have been a victorious coup had turned
into a massacre. Only a handful of the attackers had managed to escape from the Presidential Palace.

Our reinforcements were scheduled to arrive on the 15th.
We waited for hours but no one came. They arrived the
following day, exhausted, saying that unexpected events
had delayed their departure. They came in trucks owned
by a rice planter who later became so frightened lest he be
implicated in the affair that he took refuge in an embassy,
then departed for Costa Rica, and returned to Cuba as a
hero aboard a plane carrying some arms. His name: Hubert
Matos.[8]

Only 30 of the 50-man troop were armed; they had two
machine-gun rifles, a Madzen and a Johnson. The few
months spent in the Sierra had turned us into full-fledged
veterans, and the new troop, as we viewed it, had as many
defects as our original *Granma* troop: no discipline, lack of
decision, and inability to adapt to the new surroundings.
The group, led by Captain Sotús, was divided into five
squads, each composed of ten men led by a lieutenant.
Rank had been conferred by the organization in the city,
pending ratification. Squad leaders included Domínguez,
later killed at Pino del Agua; René Latour, guerrilla
organizer in the plains, killed close to the end of the war;
"Pedrín" Soto, our old *Granma* comrade who had joined us
at last, later killed in combat at the Frank País Second
Front and awarded the rank of Major posthumously; Pena,
a student from Santiago who reached the rank of Major
(he committed suicide some time after the triumph of the

Revolution); and Lieutenant Hermo, the only group leader who survived the two-year war.

Our greatest problem was our inability to walk. Jorge Sotús, the chief, was the worst offender—he was always at the rear, setting a horrible example. I had been ordered to take command but when I told Sotús he said that he had orders to turn the troop over to Fidel and no one else, that he was my commander, and so on. I still had a complex about being a foreigner and did not wish to resort to extreme measures, although it was easy to see that the men were not at ease. Following a few short marches, which seemed terribly long due to the men's lack of training, we came to the place where we were to have our rendezvous with Fidel Castro. There we met the men who had become separated from Fidel: Manuel Fajardo, Guillermo García, Juventino, Pesant, the three Sotomayor brothers and Ciro Frías.

The contrast between the two groups was tremendous. Ours was well disciplined, compact and hardened. Theirs was suffering from the usual ills: they were not accustomed to eating only one meal a day; if they found the meal unpalatable, they refused to eat. Their knapsacks were loaded with useless items, and to make them lighter they would rather get rid of a can of condensed milk than a towel (this is practically high treason in guerrilla warfare!). So we made it a point to follow their trail and pick up any food they discarded. Once we settled in our camp, there was a tense period arising from constant friction between the troop and Sotús—quite an authoritarian who lacked the gift of getting along with others. We were forced to take special measures, and René Ramos, whose *nom de guerre* was Daniel, to avoid trouble took charge of the machine-gun squad at the exit of our hideout.

Sometime later, Sotús was sent to Miami on a special mission. There he betrayed the Revolution when he met Felipe Pazos,[9] whose boundless ambition for power made him drop his commitments and appoint himself interim president, in a shoddy maneuver in which the U.S. State Department played a major role.

As time went by Captain Sotús showed signs of rehabilitation and Raúl Castro offered him his chance; the Revolution has always given everyone a chance. However, he began to plot against the Revolutionary Government. He was sentenced to 20 years' imprisonment, but aided by a prison guard, he escaped to the counter-revolutionaries' lair, the United States.

But let us get back to our story. We tried to help Sotús, easing the tension between him and the men, and explaining the need for discipline. Guillermo García went to Caracas zone, looking for Fidel, and I made a little tour to pick up Ramiro Valdés, whose leg had healed partially. Fidel arrived on the night of March 24. He and his 12 stalwart comrades were an impressive sight. What a contrast between these men, with their long beards and their makeshift packs, and the new arrvials wearing clean uniforms, carrying well-made packs, and all clean shaven! I made a full report of our problems and we held council to decide on future action. Members of the council included Fidel, Raúl, Almeida, Jorge Sotús, Ciro Frías, Guillermo García, Camilo Cienfuegos, Manuel Fajardo and I. Fidel criticized my behavior for not exerting my authority, leaving it in the hands of Sotús, a newcomer—although there was no feeling of animosity toward him—whose attitude, in Fidel's judgment, should never have been condoned. New platoons were organized, comprising the entire troop, to form three groups commanded by captains Raúl Castro, Juan Almeida and Jorge Sotús. Camilo Cienfuegos led the vanguard and Efigenio Ameijeiras the rear guard. My position: Staff Physician. Universo Sánchez was appointed Staff squad leader.

The new arrivals added to our troop's effectiveness. We also acquired two machine-gun rifles, even though they were old and badly worn. Nevertheless, we now constituted a considerable force. We studied our next step. My opinion was to attack the nearest post we could find. That would be a good test for the new men. Fidel and the others of the council were of the opinion that the men should march for long periods, to become accustomed to the rigors of jungle and mountain life as well as long treks over rugged hills. We held a short, elementary guerrilla training practice, and departed due East. Our plan was to cover long distances, looking for some group of soldiers to pounce upon.

Full of enthusiasm, we marched on to carry out our plan. The climax was to come at the battle of El Uvero.

9

Forging the Temper

The months of March and April 1957 were devoted to the reorganization and training of the rebel troops. Our army was made up of 80 men, distributed in the following manner:

The four-man vanguard was led by Camilo. Raúl Castro led a platoon of three squads, each under the command of a lieutenant; they were Julio Díaz, Ramiro Valdés, and Nano Díaz. The two comrades named Díaz were not related. Both were killed in the battle of El Uvero. Nano was from Santiago, and today the Díaz brothers' refinery in Santiago bears his name and the name of his brother, who was murdered in Santiago de Cuba. Julio was from Artemisa, a veteran of the *Granma* and of the Moncada. Jorge Sotús' lieutenants were Ciro Frías, killed at the Frank País Front; Guillermo García, now Chief of the Army of the Western Sector, and René Ramos Latour, killed while holding the rank of Major. Then came the Staff, or General Command, led by Fidel as Commander-in-Chief, and including Ciro

Redondo, Manuel Fajardo (now a Major), Crespo (Major), Universo Sánchez (now a Commander), and myself as physician.

The platoon that usually followed the column was led by Almeida as captain, and lieutenants Hermo, Guillermo Domínguez (killed at Pino del Agua), and Pena. The rear guard was led by Lieutenant Efigenio Ameijeiras and included three other men.

We learned to cook by squads. Our group was so large that the squad system allowed for a better distribution of food, medicine and ammunition. There was a veteran in most squads, teaching the new men the art of cooking and how to get the best nourishment out of our foodstuffs. They also trained the men in packing knapsacks and the correct way of walking through the Sierra.

It would take an automobile only a few hours to cover the distance between the right hill of El Lomón and El Uvero. For us, it meant weeks of slow walking, taking every precaution, while training the men for coming battles as well as for a new life. We came to Altos de Espinosa and we, the veterans, set up a guard of honor by the grave of Julio Zénon. I found a piece of the blanket I had left behind during my "strategic retreat" and shoved it into my pack, swearing that I would never again lose my equipment that way.

Paulino was my new assistant. He helped in the transportation of medicines and thus permitted me to devote a few minutes every day to attending the men. We passed Caracas hill, recalling our encounter with the enemy air force thanks to Eutimio's treachery, and found a rifle which one of our men must have left there the day of the attack. We no longer had a surplus of rifles; on the contrary, we needed more.

We had entered a new stage. A qualitative change had taken place. Throughout a wide zone, the enemy was careful not to come face to face with us; of course, we were not too eager to meet them, either. The political situation showed evident signs of opportunism. Pardo Llada, Conte Agüero[10] and other characters like them, made long-winded speeches, reeking with demagoguery, calling for harmony and peace, and timidly criticizing the government. The peace government had spoken; the new Prime Minister, Rivero Agüero, had made a pledge to go to the Sierra if necessary to bring peace to the country. However, a few days later, Batista declared that there was no need to speak with Fidel or the rebels; Fidel was not in the Sierra, and therefore there was no point in talking with a "bunch of bandits."

Thus Batista showed his determination to carry on the fight at any cost—the only point on which we whole-heartedly agreed. Colonel Barreras was then named Chief of Operations. Barreras was famous for embezzling funds from the soldiers' rations. Later he was appointed military attaché to Venezuela, and when the Batista regime came to an end, he was still sitting comfortably in his office in Caracas.

Among us at the time were three pleasant characters who provided our movement with advertising service of a sort, especially in the United States. Two of them gave us some trouble, too. They were three Yankee boys who lived in the Guantánamo Naval Base and had left to join our struggle. Two of them never heard a shot in the Sierra; worn out by the climate and privation, they asked newsman Bob Taber to take them back. The third fought in the battle of El Uvero and later retired, quite ill, but at least he did participate in a battle. The boys were ideologically unprepared for a revolution; all they did was to give vent to their spirit of adventure while in our company. We felt a sort of affection for them, but we were glad to see them go. I was especially glad, because as physician I was constantly busy with their various maladies. They simply could not stand the rigors of our campaign.

It was at that time that the government took a group of newsmen for an airplane ride over the Sierra Maestra to

prove there was nobody down there. It was a bizarre operation and it convinced no one. This was another of the
methods used by Batista's government to deceive public
opinion, aided by all the Conte Agüeros, disguised as revolutionaries, who made daily speeches in a vain effort to fool
the people.

I must mention here that at last I was going to get a
canvas hammock. This was a royal gift, which I had not yet
been awarded; in keeping with the guerrilla law, a canvas
hammock went to those who had already made their own
out of burlap sacks. Anyone could make himself a burlap
hammock, thus becoming a candidate for the next canvas
hammock, but the lint made my asthma worse, and I was
forced to sleep on the ground. Not having a burlap hammock, I was not entitled to a canvas hammock. A really
vicious circle—one of the daily events that are part of each
man's individual tragedy.

Fidel realized my plight and broke all the rules, awarding
me the precious hammock. I will always remember that this
happened by the banks of La Plata river, the day we ate
horse meat for the first time. The horse meat was not
only a luxurious *pièce de résistance;* it was the acid test of
the capacity for adaptation. Peasant members of our guerrilla
force became quite indignant and refused to eat their por-
tion of horse meat. Some of them looked upon Manuel
Fajardo as a murderer. He had worked in a slaughterhouse,
and a great event such as the slaughtering of a horse called
for the hand of a professional.

The horse belonged to a peasant named Popa, who lived
across the river. I feel confident that, following the anti-
illiteracy campaign, Popa must be able to read and write
by now. If he ever lays his hands on the magazine *Verde
Olivo,* where these notes were originally published, he will
undoubtedly recall the night when three murderous-looking
guerrilla fighters knocked at his door, mistook him for an
informer, and, adding insult to injury, took his old, moth-
eaten horse, which a few hours later was to become a meal

of exquisite taste for some of us and a test for the prejudiced bellies of the peasants, who felt that they were committing an act of cannibalism by chewing on their old friend.

10

A Famous Interview

By the middle of April 1957 we returned to the area of Palma Mocha, near Turquino Peak. Most valuable for that type of mountain warfare were our men of peasant extraction.

Guillermo García and Ciro Frías, leading groups of peasants, went back and forth, scouting, foraging for food, and catching up on the latest news; they were a real mobile vanguard. When we reached Arroyo del Infierno, all the peasants came out to welcome us and tell us about the attack—who had guided the soldiers to our hideout, number of casualties, etc. They were experts at relaying information.

Fidel did not have a radio then and he asked a peasant to lend him his. This way we could hear the news direct from Havana. The so-called press guarantees had been re-established and the newscasts were a little more informative.

Guillermo García, wearing the uniform of a corporal of the Batista forces and accompanied by two peasants, went out to look for an informer. They got their man and told him that "the Colonel wanted to see him." When he saw us, he realized that everything was lost. Cynically he told us about his liaison with the army, and how he had told "that s.o.b. Casillas" that he would guide the soldiers to where we were hiding, but that no one had paid any attention to him. A few days later, the informer was executed.

We received a message from Celia telling us that two U.S. reporters were on their way to interview Fidel about the young "gringos" who had been with us. She also sent some money donated by sympathizers of the Movement.

We decided that Sardiñas, who knew the Estrada Palma zone well, would be the guide for the newsmen. We had been devoting all our time to making contact with peasants, thus creating contact centers and permanent camps, and increasing our zone of operations. We already had several places where we could store our provisions; they were also used as relay points for messengers all over the Sierra.

People of the Sierra have an extraordinary capacity for covering long distances in the shortest possible time. We were always fooled by their version of "a half hour's walk," or "just over the hill." This type of information is always exact—for a peasant—although their concept of time, and the meaning of an hour, are completely different from city folk's.

Three days later we received news that six people were climbing toward the zone of Santo Domingo—two women, two "gringos," and two others. However, there were some contradictory stories; it was said that the guards had been informed and were surrounding the house where the new arrivals were. News travels fast in the Sierra but it also becomes distorted. Camilo went out, leading a platoon, ready to liberate the two U.S. newsmen as well as Celia, whom we knew to be part of the group. They brought them to us safely. The false information had been caused by the movement of soldiers following a tip given by some backward peasants.

On April 23, Bob Taber and a cameraman arrived. They were accompanied by Celia Sánchez and Haydée Santamaría. There were also representatives of the Movement on the plains: "Marcos" (or "Nicaragua"), Major Iglesias (now Governor of Las Villas) who was then in charge of activities in Santiago, and Marcelo Fernández, coordinator of the Movement, later vice-president of the National Bank. The latter spoke English and was appointed interpreter.

We spent a few days in diplomatic sparring, showing the

U.S. men our strong force and evading indiscreet questions. The interviews proceeded pleasantly. They, in turn, answered our questions with a full understanding of our primitive way of life, although they never became accustomed to it. Neither did they have anything in common with us.

Our group was increased by the arrival of "El Vaquerito," the cowboy, one of the most beloved figures of our revolutionary war. He told us that he had been seeking us for over a month. He said he was a native of Camagüey, and we proceeded to interrogate him. A rudimentary course of political orientation came next; this was frequently my task. Vaquerito had no political ideas. He seemed to be a wholesome, happy boy, who looked upon the whole thing as a great adventure. He was barefoot, and Celia gave him a pair of Mexican-style shoes, elaborately engraved. With the new shoes and a big straw hat he looked like a Mexican cowboy, so he was stuck with the nickname.

Vaquerito never saw the end of the revolutionary struggle. He was killed the day before we took Santa Clara. He was the leader of the suicide platoon of Column 8. We all remember his extraordinary good humor, and his bizarre, devil-may-care attitude in the face of danger. He was an inveterate liar; his stories were always an intricate network of truth and fiction, and at the end the listener was completely unable to discern where truth ended and fiction began. But when it came to his activities in the war he was truly amazing. Beginning as a messenger, he graduated first to soldier, then to leader of a suicide platoon. The same fantastic, incredible deeds he was so fond of talking about, he repeated in the battlefield. By the time he met his death his bravery had become legendary.

Once I asked Vaquerito to tell us about his life. He began his story and, secretly, we kept track of the dates. When he finished his long, amusing tale, we asked him how old he was. He must have been about 20, but when we tallied up the various dates and countless adventures, it turned out that Vaquerito must have been hard at work five years before he was born.

Comrade "Nicaragua" brought the news that several weapons were still in Santiago, leftovers from the frustrated attack on the Palace. They included ten machine guns, 11 Johnson rifles and six "muskets," as he called them. There was more armament but the Movement was contemplating the establishment of another front in the zone of the Miranda sugar mill. Fidel opposed the plan, giving them permission to take only a few weapons and demanding that as many as possible be sent to us to reinforce our equipment. We were ready to leave to avoid coming face to face with some soldiers in the vicinity, when we decided to climb Turquino Peak. This was a symbolic gesture, to climb our highest mountain. We were now on the crest of the Sierra, very close to Turquino.

Taber's interview ended at Turquino. Moving pictures were taken which were later shown on T.V. in the United States, at a time when no one took us too seriously. For example, a peasant who joined us related that Casillas had offered him $300, a cow and a calf as reward for killing Fidel. The United States was not the only one to make mistakes on the price of our maximum leader.

Our altimeter showed that Turquino was located 1,850 meters above sea level. We had never tested the device but it seemed to work well at sea level. Curiously, this height was quite different from the one appearing on official records.

An army company was following our steps. Guillermo and a group of men went out to harass them. I was still fighting my asthma and was bringing up the rear, as usual in that case. As long as I could not go into battle, I had to surrender my Thompson sub-machine gun. It took three days to get it back and it was very unpleasant for me to go about unarmed, expecting an attack at any time.

Bob Taber and two newsmen left our column and arrived safely at Guantánamo. We went on along the Sierra and the foothills, exploring new areas, making contacts, fanning the flame of the Revolution, and increasing the legend of "the bearded ones." A new spirit permeated the Sierra. Peasants would come and greet us, no longer fearful. We, in turn, had more confidence in them. Our relative strength had increased and we felt safe against any surprise attack. We also felt that a closer bond existed between us and the peasants.

11

On the March

Throughout the first two weeks of April we marched toward our objective. Beginning near Turquino, we crossed zones that later became the locale of many battles: Santa Ana, El Hombrito, Pico Verde. We found Escuedro's house and went on to Loma del Burro. Our trip toward the East was intended to pick up some weapons sent from Santiago and hide them in the Loma del Burro zone, close to Oro de Guisa.

One night I got lost in the woods and remained lost for three days until I met some people in El Hombrito. It dawned upon me at that time that we were equipped with everything necessary for survival: oil, salt, canned food and milk, a kit for starting a fire, and a compass. Up to then, I had placed great trust in that device. Now, realizing I was lost, I used my compass but without any results. I finally came to a peasant's house where they gave me the right directions. We all learned later that in rugged places like the Sierra Maestra a compass will indicate only a general direction, but never a definite course. To set a course it is necessary to be thoroughly familiar with the area or use experienced guides. This I learned from personal experience, in the zone of El Hombrito.

My return to the column was an exciting affair. I was received with great demonstrations of affection and was told that I had just missed attending the trial of three informers, one of whom, Nápoles, had been sentenced to death. Camilo had presided over the tribunal.

I carried on my duties as a physician, and whenever we arrived at some village or hamlet the people would come to me, looking for relief. My task was monotonous. I did not have too many medicines to choose from, and most cases were quite similar, typical of life in the Sierra: toothless women, who had aged prematurely, children with tremendously swollen bellies, parasitism, rickets, and avitaminosis due to lack of vitamins. (Of course, some cases still remain, but the sons of poor women are now studying at the Camilo Cienfuegos School City; they have grown; they are healthy. Quite a contrast with the first under-nourished, puny-looking contingent that arrived at our original school city.)

I remember a small girl who kept watching me as I listened to the women who came, with an almost religious attitude, to discover the reason for their various illnesses. As the girl's mother approached my "office"—a corner of an old palm-thatched hut—the little girl said to her: "Mama, this doctor tells every one the same story."

The little girl was right. My experience as a doctor was limited; moreover, every one of them told me, unwittingly, the same horrible story. What would have happened if the doctor had tried to explain to a young mother of several children who complained of fatigue after her daily task of carrying a bucket of water from the stream to her house, that she suffered simply because she did not have enough to eat? It is useless to try to explain the reason for that fatigue to a woman of the Sierra. She will argue that she has done that kind of work "all her life" and it is only now that she gets this sudden feeling of tiredness. There is the whole sad story: People in the Sierra grow like wild flowers, unattended. Then they fade away, constantly busy at thankless tasks. As a result of daily contact with these people and their problems we became firmly convinced of the need for a complete change in the life of our people. The idea of an agrarian reform became crystal-clear. Communion with the people ceased to be a mere theory, to become an integral part of ourselves.

Guerrillas and peasants began to merge into a solid mass. No one can say exactly when, in this long process, the ideas became reality and we became a part of the peasantry. As far as I am concerned, the contact with my patients in the Sierra turned a spontaneous and somewhat lyrical decision into a more serene force, one of an entirely different value. Those poor, suffering, loyal inhabitants of the Sierra cannot even imagine what a great contribution they made to the forging of our revolutionary ideology.

Guillermo García was promoted to captain, taking command of all new peasants joining the columns. Perhaps Comrade Guillermo has forgotten the date of his promotion, but it is right here in my notebook: May 6, 1957.

Haydée Santamaría left the following day. Fidel had given her instructions to establish all the necessary contacts. Then we received the news that Major Iglesias ("Nicaragua") had been arrested. He was supposed to bring the weapons and now we were at a complete loss, not knowing what to do. Still, we continued on our way.

We came to a small depression near Pino del Agua, at the very edge of the Sierra, where there were two abandoned huts. One of our patrols captured an army corporal. He was known for his many crimes dating back to Machado's regime,[11] and a few of us suggested that he be executed, but Fidel refused. We simply left him in the custody of the new recruits, who did not even have rifles, warning him that any attempt to escape would mean death.

Most of us went ahead to see if the weapons had arrived. It was a long walk, even though we did not carry packs, having left them at the camp. We did not find the weapons and of course we put the blame on Nicaragua's arrest. We were able to purchase some food and return with our load.

Not the load the men had been expecting, but a welcome one just the same.

We returned slowly, bordering the crests and being very careful in the open spaces. We heard shots ahead and became alarmed because one of our men had gone ahead to reach the camp as soon as possible. He was Lieutenant Guillermo Domínguez, recently arrived with the men from Santiago. We prepared for a fight and sent out a scouting party. It returned with Fiallo, a comrade from Crescencio's group. He came from our base camp and said that he had seen a dead man on the road. He added that there had been an encounter with some guards who had withdrawn toward Pino del Agua, where there was a large detachment of troops. We moved forward and came upon the body of the dead man.

It was Guillermo Domínguez. His body was naked from the waist up, showing a bullet wound in the left elbow and a bayonet wound in the chest. A shotgun blast had literally blown his head apart. Apparently, he had been killed with his own gun. Several buckshot pellets were clearly visible around his head.

It seems that the guards were looking for their comrade, our prisoner, and heard Domínguez coming. He must have been quite confident because he had made the same tour the day before. He was captured by the soldiers at the time that Crescencio's men were on their way to us. Crescencio's group came upon the soldiers from the rear and began firing. Then the soldiers killed Domínguez and escaped.

Pino del Agua is a sawmill camp up in the Sierra, and the road taken by the soldiers was an old lumber trail that we had to follow for 100 yards before reaching our narrow trail. Our comrade had not taken the necessary precautions and it was his luck to meet the soldiers on the lumber trail. This served as a lesson to all of us.

12

The Arms Arrive

Near Pino del Agua sawmill we killed the horse that had belonged to our prisoner, the corporal. It was a magnificent animal, but certainly of no use to us in the jungle, and we were short of food. There is a touch of irony in this story. The corporal had repeated insistently that the horse belonged to a friend of his. Now, sitting on the ground and drinking horse soup, he still kept repeating his friend's name and address should we ever have an opportunity to return the horse.

We heard over the radio that our *Granma* comrades had been sentenced and that one of the judges had voted against the verdict. He was Urrutia,[12] whose honest gesture was rewarded by his subsequent appointment as interim president of the new Republic. In itself, his vote was no more than an honest gesture—as undoubtedly it was at the time. But it led to the inauguration of a bad president, incapable of understanding the political process that was to follow, nor the depth of a revolution not made to fit his reactionary mentality. His character, and his reluctance to take a determined stand, caused plenty of trouble. The climax came when, faced by the people's unanimous hostility, he presented his resignation as president of the Republic. It happened when the people of Cuba were preparing for their first 26th of July celebration.

One day, Andrés, a contact man from Santiago, arrived with the welcome news that the arms would be delivered within a few days. A sawmill on the coast was set for the rendezvous. The Babún brothers, who owned the sawmill, were handling the operation. They expected great profit from their participation in the Revolution. Further events made them drift apart, and three of the sons of a member of the Babún firm attained the dubious privilege of being part of the counter-revolutionary element captured at Playa Girón.

Curious it is to observe how at that time many people had the idea of profiting from the Revolution. They did little favors here and there, each expecting great rewards from the new State. In the Babúns' case, they expected to be rewarded by forest concessions for commercial exploitation, including the eviction of peasants, thus increasing the latifundia of the Babún household.

We now had a new addition to our group—a U.S. newsman, Andrew Saint George, Hungarian by birth. He belonged in the same class with the Babúns. He was careful to show his less dangerous side, as a mere newsman, but he was an agent for the FBI. I was appointed to take care of him because I was the only one who spoke French, none of us speaking English. In all sincerity I must say that he did not look like a dangerous character, and after our second interview he had no fear that he would be taken for an agent.

We went on, skirting Pino del Agua, to the source of the Peladero river, marching over rugged terrain and always carrying a heavy load. We continued to a stream named Del Indio, where we spent two days. Passing through small villages, we established a sort of extra-legal Revolutionary State. Sympathizers were told to report everything that went on, including, of course, any move made by the enemy. Always, we stuck to the woods. On rare occasions we would sleep in a hut close to the woods. Daytime was spent under the protection of tall trees, under a canopy of leaves, and always on guard.

Our worst enemy at that time of the year was the *macagüera,* a species of gadfly that lays its eggs on the Macagüa tree. The *macagüeras* would bite every unprotected part of the body; our skin was far from clean, and the constant scratching caused abscesses. Our legs, wrists and necks always bore marks of the *macagüera.*

On May 18 we heard about the arms and what they were. Everyone got very excited, because each man wanted to improve his individual armament. We all hoped to get something; either a new or a used weapon since the veterans who would be issued new weapons were to turn over their old ones. We also heard that the moving pictures shot by Bob Taber at the Sierra Maestra had been very successful in the United States. Everyone was happy, with the exception of Andrew Saint George. After all, besides being an FBI agent he was also a newsman, and he felt that he had been "scooped." The following day he left the Babún zone, aboard a yacht bound for Santiago de Cuba.

A man had deserted, and we became very alarmed because everybody knew about the new weapons. We sent patrols after him and they returned in several days with news that he had taken a boat for Santiago. We suspected he had gone to inform the authorities, but we learned later that his desertion was due to his physical and moral incapacity to face the hardships of our life. In any event, we had to take extreme precautions. Our fight to improve the physical, ideological and moral qualities of the combatants went on relentlessly, but the results were not always successful. Men would find the flimsiest excuses to request release, and if they were refused, desertion would follow. We must remember that desertion meant death, the execution to be carried out at the spot where the deserter was apprehended.

That night the arms came, and it was the most beautiful sight in the world. There they were, the instruments of death, on exhibit before the hungry eyes of every fighter: three machine guns, with their tripods; three Madzen machine-gun rifles, nine M-1 carbines, 10 Johnson automatic rifles, and 6,000 rounds of ammunition. The M-1's were allotted 45 rounds apiece, and they were distributed according to each man's merits and time spent in the Sierra. One of them went to Ramiro Valdés (now a Major) and two others were given to Camilo's advance guard. Four were to cover the tripod machine guns. One machine-gun rifle went to

Captain Jorge Sotús' platoon, one to Almeida's and another to the Staff; that was my weapon. The tripod machine guns were distributed as follows: one for Raúl, another for Guillermo García, and the third for Crescencio Pérez. This was my initiation as a direct combatant. I had participated in combat, but my regular position was that of physician. For me, it was the beginning of a new stage.

I will always remember the moment when the old rifle, of inferior workmanship, was given to me. At that moment it was a precious gift. Four men had been appointed to operate the weapon. They were to follow opposite paths. The Beatón brothers, Pupo and Manolo, were executed by the Revolution for the murder of Major Cristino Naranjo and their subsequent escape to the Sierras de Oriente, where they were captured by a peasant. Another one was a 15-year-old boy who always carried the enormous weight of the gun's magazines. He is Joel Iglesias, now President of Rebel Youth, and a Major in the Rebel Army. The fourth man, now a lieutenant, was named Oñate, but we nick-named him "Cantinflas."

Our struggle to increase the ideological and combative strength of our troop, did not end with the arrival of the arms. On May 23, Fidel ordered the release of more men, among them a complete squad. This reduced our forces to 127 men, most of them armed, including 80 equipped with very good weapons.

Of the entire squad released, including its leader, only one man remained. He was Crucito, who later became one of our most beloved combatants. He was a natural poet, or balladeer, and he would hold long contests with the city poet Calixto Morales, one of the *Granma* men, who called himself "the country nightingale." Crucito would always end his songs with a scornful refrain that went something like "you old Sierra buzzard."

Crucito had written songs about the Revolution, beginning with the departure of the *Granma* from Mexico. He would sit, smoking his pipe, and compose lyrics. There was a shortage of paper in the Sierra, so Crucito learned the words by heart. Not a single line of verse remained when he was killed in the battle of Pino del Agua.

In the sawmill zone we had the invaluable aid of Enrique López, an old childhood friend of the Castros. He worked for the Babúns and was our contact man for supplies and safe travel throughout the zone. The area was crisscrossed by narrow roads that were used by the army trucks, and we had set up several ambushes but never succeeded in capturing a truck. Perhaps this contributed to the success of the coming operation which was to have the greatest psychological impact in the entire history of the war: the battle of El Uvero.

On May 25 we heard that an expeditionary group, led by Calixto Sánchez, had arrived aboard the launch *Corintia* and landed near Mayarí. A few days later we heard about the disastrous outcome of that expedition. Prío Socarrás[13] had the habit of sending his men to die, but never bothered to accompany them. On the news of the landing and its aftermath, we decided it was imperative to undertake diversions against the enemy to give the survivors a chance to reach some place where they could reorganize themselves and go into action. We did this out of sheer solidarity with the men, not knowing their social makeup nor the real purpose of the landing.

On that occasion, we held an interesting debate, with Fidel and myself the leading characters. I argued that we should not forego the opportunity to seize an army truck, that we should devote ourselves, specifically, to capture one as it went carelessly by. Fidel, on the other hand, argued for the operation of El Uvero, since the capture of the army post would have a tremendous psychological impact and the event would be known throughout the country—which would never happen if we seized a truck. That easily could be reported as a mere accident, with a few casualties. In that case, although some people might suspect the truth, nobody would know about our existence as an effective fighting force in the Sierra. This did not mean discarding the idea of seizing a truck, but this was not to be the focal point of our activities.

Now, several years after that debate where Fidel had the last word but did not convince me, I must recognize that the decision was correct; it would have been of very little advantage to us to carry out an action against a patrol traveling by truck. Of course, our desire to fight made us adopt drastic positions, lacking the patience, and perhaps even the vision, to see long-range objectives. Anyway, we had reached final preparations for the El Uvero action.

13

Battle of El Uvero

Once we had settled on our objective, the next step was to plan the attack. We had to find out about the number of soldiers, sentry posts, type of communications, access roads, civilian population and its distribution, and so on. Comrade Caldero (now a Major in the Rebel Army) did a wonderful job in this department. Caldero, I seem to remember, was the sawmill manager's son-in-law.

We assumed that the army had more or less precise information about our presence in the zone, because we had captured two informers who confessed that Casillas had sent them to pinpoint the Rebel Army's whereabouts and its meeting places. The sight of the two informers, pleading for their lives, was disgusting as well as moving, but the laws of war could not be disregarded in those difficult moments, and both men were executed.

That same day, the Staff and all the officers held a meeting. Fidel announced that we would go into action within the next 48 hours; he told us to remain fully dressed

Ernesto Che Guevara

Fidel Castro

Raúl Castro

The yacht *Granma*

Cane cutters in Oriente province during Batista's regime.

Fidel Castro with Haydée Santamaría and Celia Sánchez
in the Sierra.

Comandante Camilo Cienfuegos (*waving*).

Che Guevara addressing the
United Nations.

A view of the memorial service in honor of Che Guevara, in Havana,
October 18, 1967.

"New cries of battle and victory."

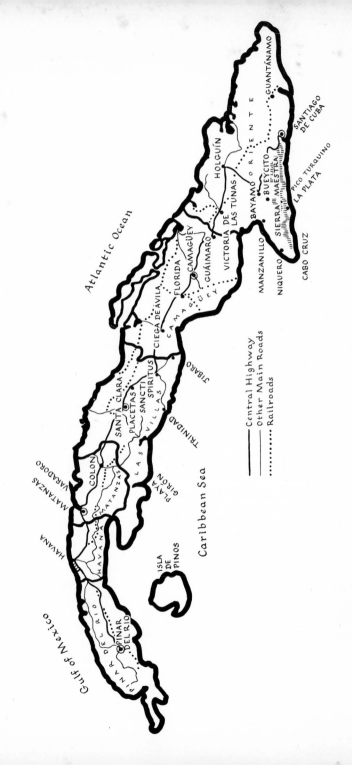

and equipped, ready to leave. No instructions were given at the time.

Caldero was to be the guide. He knew the post at El Uvero, every way in and out, and every access road. We started at night. It was a long march, about 10 miles, but, luckily, all downhill along the roads built by the Babúns. Yet it took us about eight hours to cover the distance, because of the extreme precautions taken as we neared the danger zone. Finally, the orders came, and they were very simple: take the sentry posts and riddle the wooden structure holding the garrison.

We knew that the post had no major defenses except for a few logs distributed around the building. The strong points were the sentry posts, of four soldiers each, placed strategically outside the building. Our Staff was to be established atop a hill overlooking the post, a good vantage point from which to direct the action. It was easy to approach within close range of the post by crawling through the dense woods. We had strict orders not to shoot toward the civilian area where women and children lived. The manager's wife, who knew of our plan, also lived there, but she had refused to leave so as not to arouse suspicion. The civilians were uppermost in our minds as we took our positions to begin the attack.

El Uvero post was located at the very edge of the water so we had to attack only three sides.

Platoons led by Jorge Sotús and Guillermo García were sent to the spot overlooking the road running alongside the coast. It was Almeida's job to liquidate the sentry post facing the mountain, more or less to the North; Fidel was to be at the hill overlooking the post, and Raúl was to make a frontal attack. I was assigned an intermediate post with my machine-gun rifle and my aides. Camilo and Ameijeiras were to attack from the front, between my position and Raúl's, but they lost their way in the dark and began the attack at my left. Crescencio Pérez' platoon was to advance along the road leading to Chivirico and stop any reinforcements coming that way.

We expected the attack to be of short duration, due to the element of surprise, but minutes went by and we still could not place our men in the ideal positions. Our guides—Caldero and one of the zone's guides, Eligio Mendoza—went back and forth with reports. Soon it would be daybreak and the planned surprise attack seemed doomed to failure. Jorge Sotús sent word that he was having trouble pinpointing his target, but it was too late to figure out new maneuvers. When Fidel opened fire with his rifle we were able to locate the post by the flashes of the soldiers' rifles. I was up on an elevated area and was able to see the post, but the distance was too great and we moved in, looking for a better position.

Everybody was advancing. Almeida was headed for the sentry post covering the entrance, and on my left I could see Camilo's cap, with a piece of cloth sticking from the back, Foreign-Legion style, but bearing the insignia of the Movement. We continued to advance, amidst heavy gunfire, taking all the necessary precautions.

We began to receive reinforcements, men who had become separated from their units. A comrade nicknamed "Bomba," Mario Leal, and Acuña, joined our small group. The soldiers were putting up a stiff resistance and now we had reached the flat, open spaces where we had to be very wary of the enemy's accurate fire. I was about 50 or 60 yards from their advance guard and saw two soldiers come out of a trench. I fired, but they took refuge in one of the houses. Firing toward the houses was out of the question, so we kept pressing forward across open ground with the bullets whizzing by. I heard someone moaning and I thought perhaps he had a wound in his head. I made a quick inspection: the bullet had hit Leal on the temple. He was fainting and his side was paralyzed; I can't recall whether it was the left or right side. The only "bandage" I could lay my hands on was a piece of paper, so I placed it on the wound. Joel

Iglesias came to help Leal, while we continued the attack.
A few seconds later, Acuña fell. We could no longer
advance, and we kept firing toward a trench and getting
plenty of return fire. We were gathering our courage for a
final attack as the only way left to overcome the enemy's
resistance. At that very moment the post surrendered.

It takes only a few minutes to describe the battle, but the
actual time was two hours and 45 minutes, counting from
the opening shot to the time we entered the post. On my
right—I believe it was Víctor Mora and other comrades—
had captured several soldiers who had put up a last struggle.
A soldier came out of the trench in front of us, holding out
his weapon in a gesture of surrender. We could hear cries
of surrender coming from all sides. We ran toward the
building and there was a burst of machine-gun fire. It was
that last burst that killed Lieutenant Nano Díaz.

Reaching the civilian area, we captured the two soldiers
who had escaped my fire, and also the post physician and
his assistant. A curious incident occurred, involving the
physician, a calm, gray-haired man whom I never saw
again. I do not know if he is now part of our Revolution. I
was never too much of a physician and the number of
wounded men being carried in was growing. Moreover, I
was not too inclined to medicine at the moment. When I
went to turn the wounded over to the army physician he
asked me how old I was and the date of my graduation. I
told him I had several years' experience and he said: "Look,
you take care of this; I just graduated and I have very little
experience." His lack of practice and his fear at finding
himself a prisoner made him forget whatever he knew about
his profession. From that moment, I had to exchange my
soldier's uniform for a physician's robe; actually, all I did
was wash my hands.

Following the combat, one of the bloodiest we ever had,
we began to gather data and now I am able to present a
more general picture; up to now the story was based on my
personal experience. What happened was more or less as

follows. When Fidel opened fire, giving the signal to begin, everybody began to attack the pre-determined objectives, and the army returned the fire, especially toward the hill where Fidel was. Julito Díaz was killed, standing next to Fidel. The soldiers' resistance was increasing and it was practically impossible to press on toward our goal. The most important task had been given to Almeida, at the center. He was to liquidate the sentry post to open the way for his men and Raúl's. We were told how Eligio Mendoza, the guide, had grabbed a rifle and joined the attack. He was a very superstitious man, and when he was warned to take care of himself he scornfully replied that his "saint" would take care of that. A few seconds later, he was practically cut in two by a burst of machine-gun fire. The enemy's fire was heavy and we lost a few men.

We were finding it very difficult to gain any distance through the center. Jorge Sotús, on the road to Peladero, tried a flank maneuver, accompanied by his assistant, nicknamed "The Policeman," who was killed almost immediately, and Sotús had to dive into the sea to escape. Others in his platoon made an effort to advance but were repelled. A peasant, Vegas, was killed; Manals was hit in the lungs; Quike Escalona was hit in the arm, hand and buttocks. Hiding behind the log barricade, the soldiers were cutting our small troop to pieces. Almeida called for a final attack to take the enemy position. Cilleros, Maceo, Hermes Leyva and Pena were wounded, and Almeida himself was hit in the left leg and shoulder. Moll was killed. However, this last rush overran the sentry post and opened the way to the fort. On the other side, Guillermo García's accurate machine-gun fire had killed three soldiers; another tried to escape and was also killed. Raúl, his platoon divided into two groups, began a rapid advance toward the post. It was the attack carried out by Guillermo García and Almeida that turned the tide; they liquidated their respective enemy posts, allowing for the final attack. A praiseworthy performance was that of Luis Crespo, who left the Staff to join the fight.

As we reached the building, where somebody was waving a white handkerchief, one of our men must have fired and the enemy replied with a burst that killed Nano Díaz, who had been using his machine gun very effectively against the soldiers. Crescencio's platoon was practically out of action due to a jammed machine gun, so they continued covering the road from Chivirico, and captured two soldiers who had tried to escape along that road. The battle lasted two hours and 45 minutes and no civilians were hurt, despite the intense fire.

Our casualties were: Moll, Nano Díaz, Vega, "The Policeman," Julito Díaz and Eligio Mendoza, dead; Leal and Cilleros, badly wounded. Others, more or less seriously wounded, were Maceo, hit on the shoulder; Hermes Leyva, surface wound in the chest; Quike Escalona, right arm and hand; Pena, shot in the knee; Manuel Acuña, right arm; and Manals shot in the lungs, no other symptoms. A total of 15 comrades out of action. The enemy had 19 wounded, 14 dead; 14 were captured and six had escaped. A total of 53 men, they were commanded by a second lieutenant who had raised the white flag after he was wounded.

We had 80 men, and the enemy 53; a total of 133, with 38—over one-fourth—out of action in less than two and a half hours' fighting. It had been a reckless, wide-open attack upon an enemy who was badly protected, and we must admit that both sides showed tremendous courage. For us it was a victory that meant that our guerrillas had reached full maturity. From that moment, our morale increased enormously, our determination and hope for victory also grew, and although the months that followed were a hard test, we now had the key to the secret of how to beat the enemy. This battle sealed the fate of every garrison located far from large concentrations of troops, and every small army post was soon dismantled.

One of the very first shots fired in the combat had cut off telephone communications with Santiago, and the enemy recognizance planes arrived hours later, when we had already reached the mountains. The following will give an idea of the concentrated fire we had poured into the army post: in addition to the 14 dead soldiers there were three dead parakeets—the guards had five of these as pets—and it must have taken a veritable deluge of bullets to hit creatures so small.

My return to the medical profession had its sad moments. My first patient was Cilleros. A bullet had broken his right arm, went through his lungs and was imbedded in his spine, paralyzing his legs. His condition was very serious, and all I could do was give him some drugs and bandage his chest tightly so that he could breath a little more comfortably. We tried to save his life by doing the only thing we could do at the time—take the 14 prisoners with us and leave our two wounded men, Leal and Cilleros, with the enemy, under the guarantee of the doctor's word of honor. When I told Cilleros about our decision, adding a few words of comfort, he looked at me with a sad smile on his lips that was more eloquent than words. He knew this was the end. We knew it, too, and I was tempted to kiss him on the forehead but I realized that it would mean signing his death sentence. It was my duty not to make his last moments any worse by an act that would only confirm what he already suspected. I said a fond goodbye to my two comrades. They insisted on staying with us even if it meant death for them, but it was our duty to fight for their lives to the last minute. We left them there, fraternizing with the wounded soldiers, who had also been attended to the best of our ability.

Our comrades were treated very decently by the enemy soldiers, but Cilleros never reached Santiago. The other survived, and was sent to the Isle of Pines prison. He still bears the marks of that important episode of our revolutionary war.

We loaded one of Babúns' trucks with every sort of item,

principally medicines, and went on to our hideout in the mountains where we arrived in time to attend the wounded and pay our last respects to the dead. Expecting the army would be in hot pursuit, we decided that everyone who was able to walk was to go as far as possible from the place. The wounded were to remain with me. Enrique López was to find transportation, a hideout, a few helpers to carry the wounded and contact-men to bring medicine.

Throughout the night we kept discussing the battle. No one slept, and all had something to say about what they had seen or done. Out of curiosity I kept a record of the enemy dead and wounded, according to the story-tellers, and they seemed to surpass the actual number of enemy soldiers. Each man's story touched the realm of fantasy. This and other experiences like it taught us that all data should be checked and re-checked by several persons. In our exaggerated eagerness for accuracy, we went so far as to demand physical proof, such as items taken from an enemy soldier, before we counted him as an enemy loss. Our main concern was to broadcast the truth. This was the central theme of all information given by the Rebel Army and we made every effort to make our comrades realize how important it was to have respect for truth, and to under-stand that truth was to be placed above transitory victory.

At dawn, we bade farewell to the victorious troops. I remained with Joel Iglesias, Oñate, a guide named Sinecio Torres and Vilo Acuña (now a Major in the Rebel Army), who stayed to take care of his uncle.

14

Nursing the Wounded

The day following the Uvero battle we could see enemy planes circling by. They had been at it since dawn. Once we said goodbye to the comrades, we began to erase every trace of our entrance into the woods. We were only 100 yards away from a road, and were waiting for Enrique López to begin the transfer of our wounded men.

Almeida, Pena, Escalona and Manals were unable to walk. Manuel Acuña, Hermes Leyva and Maceo could move about with difficulty. Vilo Acuña, the guide Sinecio Torres, Joel Iglesias, Alejandro Oñate and I were to protect, transport and nurse them. Hours later, someone came to tell us that Enrique López could not help us; his daughter was ill and he had to leave for Santiago. He was to send us some volunteers but they never showed up.

It was a serious situation. Escalona's wound was infected and we could not tell how badly Manals was hurt. We scouted the nearby roads and found no soldiers, so we decided to take them to an abandoned hut located two or three miles away where there were plenty of chickens.

Two of the sawmill workers helped us carry the wounded, who had been placed in hammocks. The following day, after a good chicken dinner, we left the place. We had remained practically in the same spot, too near the roads that could be used by enemy soldiers. We started our short but very difficult journey toward a ravine called Del Indio. We crossed it and then climbed to a hut owned by a peasant, Israel, who lived with his wife and a brother-in-law. It was a rough trip but we finally made it. Those wonderful people even offered us the couple's bed so that our wounded men could get some sleep.

We had left some weapons at our former camp, most of

them in bad condition. There were other implements, too, that we had to abandon as the weight of the wounded men made travel increasingly difficult. It seemed that we always left something behind in some hut or camp, and we wanted to get back this time and erase all signs that might lead to us. Our lives depended on it. At the same time, Sinecio the guide went to get some friends of his who lived in the zone of Peladero.

Acuña and Joel said they had heard strange voices on the other side of the mountain. We thought the time had come to put up a fight, since our duty was to defend our precious load of wounded comrades. We went ahead wanting the encounter to take place as far as possible from the hut. We found prints of bare feet on the same trail we had used before. Then we heard the voices of men apparently engaged in careless conversation. I had my machine gun ready and, flanked by Vilo and Joel, I came upon the group. They were the prisoners Fidel had set free at El Uvero and they were looking for a way out of the woods. Most of them were barefoot, and an old corporal, practically exhausted, expressed his admiration for us and for our expertness in moving about the woods. They had no guide; all they had was a pass, signed by Fidel. Taking advantage of the great impression we had made upon them, we warned them not to enter the woods again.

We spent the night in the hut. At dawn we returned to the woods and sent the peasant to catch some chickens for the wounded men. We waited the entire day for him and his wife but they never returned. Some time later, we heard they had been arrested and the soldiers had forced them to guide them to our camp. Fortunately, we had moved out one day before.

We kept a strict vigilance and would never have been taken by surprise. But we could not predict the outcome of a battle under such unfavorable conditions. Sinecio returned that night with three volunteers—an old man, Feliciano, and two others who later became members of the Rebel

Army. They were Banderas, who was killed in the battle of Jigüe, holding the rank of lieutenant, and Israel Pardo, the oldest member of a large family of fighters; he is now a captain. These men helped us transfer the wounded to another hut while Sinecio awaited the peasants who were to bring our food. Of course, we did not know that they had been arrested. We suspected a trap, and made up our minds to leave our new hideout. We ate a frugal meal consisting of some vegetables dug from around the hut. The following day, six months after the *Granma* landing, we were on our way. Each stage of our march was short, and incredibly tiring, even for one accustomed to mountain traveling. We could carry only one hammock which had to be tied to a strong branch and borne on the shoulders of two or four men. The branch would literally tear the bearer's shoulders to pieces, so every ten minutes or so we had to change carriers. Six or eight men are needed to carry a wounded person in this manner. Almeida half-walked, half-dragged himself along from tree to tree until Israel made a short cut through the woods and we met the bearers.

We arrived at the Pardos' at dusk, following a terrible rainstorm. It had taken us 12 hours to cover a distance of three miles.

Sinecio was our salvation. He knew every road and every person in the zone. It was he who managed to get Manals out and send him to Santiago, and we were getting ready to send Escalona too, as his wound were still badly infected. We heard all sorts of contradictory news: Celia Sánchez had been arrested; Celia Sánchez had been killed, and so on. It was said that an army patrol had captured Hermes Caldero. We did not know what to believe, and some of the reports were really frightening, since Celia, for example, was our only safe, confidential contact. Her arrest would mean isolation for all of us. Fortunately, the news about Celia turned out to be false. Hermes, however, was arrested and managed to survive a long jail sentence.

David, a foreman for one of the landowners, was very

helpful. He had slaughtered a cow for us near the coast, and we had to go and bring in the pieces. This had to be done at night and I sent a group of men led by Israel Pardo, and a second group led by Banderas. Banderas was quite undisciplined and he made the men carry the entire load. It took them all night to bring the meat. A small troop was being organized, which I was to lead since Almeida was hurt. Aware of my responsibility, I told Banderas he was no longer a combatant, that unless he improved his behavior he was to remain as a sympathizer. He did improve, although he was no model of discipline; but he was an alert man, of great ingenuity, and he had come face to face with reality through the medium of the Revolution. He had been working a small parcel of land wrested from the woods, and lived in a small hut with two little pigs and a dog. One day he showed me his sons' photograph; they lived with his ex-wife in Santiago. Banderas said he hoped that once the Revolution had succeeded, he could go somewhere to work a piece of good land, not this inhospitable scrap of land practically hanging from the Sierra. The man had a passion for agriculture.

I told him about cooperatives, but he was unable to understand. He wanted to work the land by himself and for himself. Gradually, he began to understand the advantage of collective work, the use of farm machinery, etc. Banderas would have been a vanguard fighter in agricultural production. In the Sierra, he improved his reading and writing and he really was preparing for the future. He was a wide-awake peasant who knew the value of self-sacrifice when it comes to writing a new page in history.

I held a long conversation with David, the foreman. He was on his way to Santiago and he wanted a list of things we needed, so that he could get them for us. He was the typical foreman, faithful to his boss, with a great scorn for peasants, and a racist to boot. However, when the army arrested and tortured him, his main concern when he saw us again was to explain that he had refused to talk. I do not know if David is still in Cuba; perhaps he followed his bosses, whose possessions were confiscated by the Revolution. I must say he was a man who, at that moment, felt the need for change; he felt that change was certain to come, although he never imagined it might reach him and his world. The structure of the Revolution is based upon many sincere efforts made by humble men; our mission is to bring out the best in everyone and turn everyone into a revolutionary. The Revolution is made up of Davids who did not understand too well, of Banderas who did not live to see the dawn, of blind sacrifices, of unrewarded sacrifices.

We who are able to witness the Revolution's accomplishments must remember those who fell by the roadside, and do our utmost to decrease the number of laggards.

15

The Return

We spent the entire month of June 1957 nursing the wounded of the Uvero battle and organizing the small group that was to join Fidel's column.

David was our contact man with the outside. His timely advice, in addition to the food he always managed to find, made our situation quite bearable. We did not know Pancho Tamayo then. Old Pancho, a peasant, was another contact man and his cooperation will always be remembered. Pancho was killed by the Beatóns,[14] after the triumph of the Revolution.

Sinecio began to show a lack of revolutionary morals. He used the Movement's funds to get drunk, he would not obey orders, and once, following one of his escapades, he brought back 11 unarmed men. We tried to avoid enlistment of unarmed men, but the peasants kept bringing more and more young men who were anxious to join us. Our column was visited by more than 40 people, but on the other hand, desertions continued, with or without our permission, so our effective troops never amounted to more than 30 men.

My asthma became worse and I was reduced to immobility, like the wounded. I used to relieve my condition by smoking the dry leaf of the *clarín*, the Sierra's remedy, until we received the medicines and I was able to recuperate, but our departure was still postponed.

We organized a group to recover all the weapons damaged after the Uvero attack; we could still repair them and put them back into use. In our position, those old rifles, more or less serviceable and including a 30-caliber machine gun, became a potential treasure, and we spent a whole night looking for them. Finally, our departure was set for June 24. This was our army: five men still recovering from their wounds, five assistants, 10 new men from Bayamo, two that had recently joined because they "felt like it," and four others from that zone—total: 26. We started out with Vilo Acuña in the advance guard, followed by the Commanding Staff which I led because Almeida could hardly walk, and two other squads led by Maceo and Pena. Pena was a lieutenant; Maceo and Vilo soldiers, and the highest rank was held by Almeida, who was a captain. We did not leave on the 24th because of several incidents. A guide was supposed to come with another man, or perhaps it was a new shipment of medicine and food. Old Tamayo went back and forth bringing news, canned food and clothing. We had to find a cave to store food. Our contacts in Santiago had materialized and David had brought back such a big load that nobody could carry it, at least not our troop made up of convalescents and raw recruits.

On June 26 I made my debut as dentist, and in the Sierra I became known by the modest title of "tooth-puller." My first victim was Israel Pardo (now a Captain in the army) who did not fare too badly. The second was Joel Iglesias and I thought that if I ever extracted his ailing canine tooth I would have to use a stick of dynamite. I must confess that I failed, and Joel finished the war with the tooth still in his mouth. My lack of experience and of anesthetic forced me to resort to "psychological" anesthesia, which in plain language means insulting the patients whenever they complained about the pain.

Whenever we announced our departure someone would desert, only to be replaced by newcomers. Tamayo brought four men, among them Félix Mendoza, who had a rifle. He told us the army had caught them off guard and his comrade had escaped while he had jumped off a cliff. Later, we learned that the "army" was a patrol led by Lalo Sardiñas. They found Felix's friend who became a member of Fidel's troop. Evelio Saborit (now a Major in the Rebel Army) also joined us.

With the addition of Félix Mendoza and his group, we increased our number to 36 but the next day three men left us, to be replaced by others and we went back to 35. However, as soon as we started, the number of men decreased. We were now in the foothills of Peladero, climbing a very short distance at each stage.

The news over the radio reported violence all over the island. On July 1 we heard about the death of Josué País, Frank País' brother, and others in Santiago. The city was the scene of constant struggle. Despite our short journeys, some of the new recruits began to feel depressed and asked to be sent to the city "where they could be more useful." On the way down we passed Benito Mora, at the hill known as The Bottle. He played the gracious host in his little hut perched at the edge of the Sierra. Shortly before our arrival at Benito's, I spoke to the men telling them that we were about to face difficult, dangerous days, with the enemy nearby, and that we might have to go on for several days, always on the move, with very little food. Some of them were decent enough to express their fear and leave immediately, but a man named Chicho spoke on behalf of his group, saying that they were ready to "go to their death" if necessary. Soon after our visit to Benito we camped near a stream and were greatly surprised when the same group approached and told us that they would like to leave the guerrillas. We agreed and jokingly nicknamed the stream "Death's Stream." After all, this was where Chicho and his confrères had finished their careers as guerrillas.

Now we were only 28, but the following day two new recruits, ex-army men, came to the Sierra to fight for freedom. They were Gilberto Capote and Nicolás. They were guided by Arístides Guerra, another contact man who became of inestimable value to our column. We used to call him "The Food King." The "King" helped us at all times, carrying out missions much more dangerous than fighting. Several times he drove caravans of mules from Bayamo to our zone of operations.

As we continued our short journeys we tried to train our men in the use of firearms. We appointed the two ex-army men as instructors in dismantling and putting together the weapons, dry-run firing, etc. Unfortunately, no sooner had the lessons begun when an instructor's gun went off accidentally. The man was demoted, and we began to look upon him with a certain degree of suspicion, although his look of genuine consternation made it very difficult for us not to believe he was truly sorry about the whole thing. Neither he or the other ex-army man could stand the constant moving, and they left with Arístides. Gilberto Capote did return some time later. He died a hero's death at Pino del Agua, with the rank of lieutenant.

We left the house of Polo Torres at La Mesa, which later became one of our centers of operations, and went on, guided by a peasant, Tuto Almeida. We had to reach La Nevada and join Fidel, crossing the North slope of the Turguino. On our way we spied two people who ran away when they saw us and we had to chase them for quite a distance before we caught them. They were two Negro girls, Adventists, and absolutely against any sort of violence.

However, they fully supported us then and for the duration of the war.

We ate a hearty meal and rested. Then, as we neared Malverde, which we had to cross in order to get to La Nevada, we were told that soldiers were all over the zone. Following a short meeting between our so-called Staff and the guides, we turned back and headed for the Turquino— a much rougher road, but less dangerous under the circumstances.

Our little transistor radio kept us well informed, although the news was quite alarming—heavy fighting in the Estrada Palma zone, Raúl badly wounded, etc. Now I cannot remember whether the news came from our radio or the Sierra grapevine. We did not dare credit sources that had been proven false on other occasions. We did our best to rush toward Fidel's location. Marching through the Sierra at night, we came to the house of a peasant, El Vizcaíno (the Basque), who lived in the foothills of Turquino. He lived alone in his little hut and his only friends were some books on Marxism which he kept hidden carefully away under a rock, far from the hut. He was proud of his Marxist militancy, which no one in that zone suspected. He showed us the way and we continued our slow march.

Sinecio was now getting further away from his home base and for a peasant like him, who was now practically an outlaw, the situation appeared alarming. One day, carrying a rifle, he joined another named Cuervo, who was doing sentry duty with a Remington rifle. Half an hour later I went to see what was going on; I did not trust Sinecio any longer and rifles were a treasure to be well guarded. When I reached the sentry post they were both gone. Banderas and Israel Pardo went after them, despite the fact that they had only revolvers and the two escapees had rifles. The men had disappeared.

It is hard to maintain high morale among a troop with practically no armament, in no direct contact with the head of the Revolution, stumbling through the darkness, lacking experience, surrounded by enemies who seemed giants if one were to listen to the peasants' tales. Men from the plains, unaccustomed to the rough going over mountains, added to the crisis. There was an attempt at desertion, led by the "Mexican" who reached the rank of captain but is now living in Miami, another traitor to the Revolution.

I heard about the attempted desertion from Hermes Leyva, Joel's cousin, and called for a confrontation to solve the problem. The "Mexican" swore by all his ancestors that he had no intention of leaving, that all he wanted was to lead his own guerrilla group to kill informers, because there was no action in our group. Actually, his plan was to kill informers and rob them, a typical bandit's behavior. Later, at the battle of El Hombrito, we lost only one man, Hermes Leyva. Suspicion fell upon the "Mexican," but we could never prove that he had murdered Leyva.

The "Mexican" remained, swearing on his honor as a revolutionary that he would never try to escape or encourage anyone to do so. Following a few short, tiring marches we reached the zone of Palma Mocha, on the western slope of Turquino, where we received a great welcome from the peasants and established good relations with them thanks to my new profession as "tooth-puller," which I practiced with great enthusiasm.

Once again we had a good meal and rested for a fast march toward our old friendly zones of Palma Mocha and El Infierno, where we arrived June 15. Emilio Cabrera, a peasant living in the area, reported that Lalo Sardiñas had set up an ambush nearby, involving great risk to his house in the event of a fight.

On June 16 our column met a platoon belonging to Fidel's column, led by Lalo Sardiñas. Sardiñas told us he had been forced to join the Revolution. He was a store owner who used to bring us food when we were in the plains. One day he was taken by surprise and he had to kill a man. Then he took the road to the Sierra. Now he had instructions to lie in wait for Sánchez Mosquera's column. Once again, Sánchez

Mosquera, an obstinate man, had come to Palma Mocha to find himself practically surrounded by Fidel's column. He evaded the trap and went full speed to the other side of Turquino.

We had heard about the presence of troops nearby and had seen the trenches. We did not know that what we considered signs of a sustained offensive against us was really an enemy retreat, signifying a complete qualitative change in the character of operations in the Sierra. We were now strong enough to encircle the enemy and force him to flee under the threat of complete annihilation.

The enemy learned his lesson well. The soldiers made only sporadic raids in the Sierra, but one of the most tenacious, aggressive and bloody officers of the enemy army was Sánchez Mosquera. In 1957 he was only a lieutenant; after the last battle of the general offensive by the army, which ended in defeat, he was promoted to colonel. He had a meteoric career as regards promotion. He was also extremely successful in robbing the peasants of everything they owned every time he set foot in the labyrinths of the Sierra Maestra.

16

Treason in the Making

It was a pleasure to look at our troops. Close to 200 men, well disciplined, with greater morale, and armed with good weapons, some of them new. The qualitative change I mentioned before was not quite evident in the Sierra. Here was a truly free territory, with safety measures not so necessary, and with some freedom to carry on conversations at night while resting in our hammocks. We were allowed to visit nearby villages and establish closer ties with the peasants.

We were moved by the hearty welcome given by our comrades.

Felipe Pazos and Raúl Chibás were the "prima donnas" of the moment, although they were complete opposites.[15] Raúl Chibás lived in the shadow of his brother's reputation —for Eddie Chibás was the symbol of an era—but he had none of his brother's virtues. He was neither expressive nor intelligent. Only his absolute mediocrity allowed him to be the principal figure of the Orthodox party. He spoke very little and he wanted to leave the Sierra at once.

Felipe Pazos had a certain personality. He was rated as a great economist and had a reputation as an honest person. His reputation for honesty was due to the fact that he did not steal from public funds during his term as President of the National Bank, in Prío Socarrás' regime, which was notorious for larceny and embezzlement. Many people think this was a great achievement, to remain pure throughout a regime of debauchery and thievery. He deserved credit, to be sure, but only as an official who followed his administrative career, while turning a deaf ear to the country's great problems. On the other hand, can anyone imagine a revolutionary who failed to speak up against the inconceivable excess and abuse rampant at the time? Felipe Pazos managed to keep his mouth shut, and after Batista's coup (1952) left the post of President of the National Bank, surrounded by an aura of virtue—honesty, intelligence, and great experience as an economist. Petulantly, he expected to come to the Sierra and take over. This pint-sized Machiavelli thought he was destined to control the country's future.

It is very possible that he was already planning to betray the Revolution; perhaps this came later. Yet, his position was never defined clearly.

Protected by the joint declaration which we will analyze soon, he appointed himself delegate of the July 26th Movement in Miami and he was on the verge of being appointed

Interim President of the Republic. By this maneuver, Prío made sure that he would have a faithful man within the provisional government.

We did not have much time to talk, but Fidel told me about his efforts to turn out a really militant document that would set the basis for a declaration of principles. This was a difficult task when faced by these two "stone-age" brains, immune to the call of the people's struggle.

Fundamentally, the manifesto reiterated "the establishment of a great civic revolutionary front comprising all opposition parties, all civic institutions and all revolutionary forces."

Several proposals were submitted, including "the establishment of a civic revolutionary front in a common front of struggle," the appointment of "a figure designated to preside over the provisional government." The document stated that the front neither requested nor would accept intervention by any other country in the internal affairs of Cuba. It "did not accept any military junta as a provisional government of the Republic." It stated the determination to separate the army from politics and to safeguard the armed forces against political intrigue and influence; elections were to be held within one year.

The policy of the provisional government would include freedom for all political prisoners, civilian and military; absolute guarantee of freedom of the press and radio, with all rights, individual or political, to be guaranteed by the Constitution; appointment of interim mayors in all municipalities, following consultation with the district's civic institutions; prosecution of embezzlement in all forms, and the adoption of measures aimed at increasing efficiency of all State organizations; establishment of civil service; democratization of trade-union policy, promotion of free elections in all trade unions and industrial workers' federations; beginning of an intense anti-illiteracy campaign, and public education on civic affairs, pointing out the citizens' rights and duties to society and the country. The manifesto promised "to establish the bases for an Agrarian Reform aimed at distribution of untilled lands, giving ownership to all sharecroppers, tenants and squatters having small lots of land, either private or State-owned, provided the farmer-owners are compensated." It called for establishment of a foreign policy safeguarding our currency's stability and aimed at investing the country's capital in productive works; to expedite the process of industrialization and create additional employment opportunities.

In addition, there were two points of special emphasis: "First: The need to appoint, from this moment, the person who will preside over the Provisional Government of the Republic, to prove to the entire world that Cubans can become united under a slogan of freedom; to support the person who, for his impartiality, capabilities and honesty, can personify such a slogan. There are many able men in Cuba who can preside over the Republic." Felipe Pazos, one of the co-signers, felt quite confident that there was only one man for the presidency, himself.

"Second: that this person be appointed by an ensemble of civic non-political institutions, whose support would safeguard the president from any political commitments, thus insuring clean, impartial elections."

The document also stated "it is not necessary to come to the Sierra for any discussions. We can have representatives in Havana, Mexico or wherever it becomes necessary."

Fidel had pressed for more explicit statements regarding the Agrarian Reform, but it was very difficult to crash through the wall of the two "stone-age" characters. "To establish the bases for an Agrarian Reform aimed at the distribution of untilled lands," was the kind of policy with which even the newspaper *Diario de la Marina*[16] might agree. To make it worse, there was the clause "provided the farmer-owners are compensated."

The Revolution did not comply with some of the commitments, as originally stated. We must emphasize that the enemy broke the pact expressed in the manifesto when they refused to acknowledge the authority of the Sierra and made an attempt to shackle the future revolutionary government.

We were not satisfied with the manifesto, but it was necessary; at the time, it was progressive. It could not possibly last beyond circumstances that would constitute an obstacle to the development of the revolutionary movement. In this matter, the enemy helped us break the uncomfortable bonds and gave us the opportunity to show the people what their real intentions were.

We were aware that this was a minimal program, limiting our own efforts, but we had to recognize that it was impossible to impose our will from the Sierra Maestra. For a long period of time, we would have to depend upon a succession of "friends" who were trying to use our military strength and the people's great trust in Fidel for Machiavellian maneuvers, above all, to maintain imperialist domination of Cuba with the aid of the importing bourgeoisie, closely linked with the U.S. owners.

The manifesto had its positive sides. It mentioned the Sierra Maestra and it stated clearly: "Let no one be deceived by Government propaganda about the situation in the Sierra Maestra. The Sierra Maestra is an indestructible bulwark of freedom. It is in the hearts of our people and it is here that we will know how to do justice to the faith and the confidence of our people." The words "we will know how" meant that Fidel and only Fidel knew how. The other two were incapable of following the development of the struggle in the Sierra, not even as spectators. They left the Sierra immediately. Chibás was arrested and beaten by the police. Both managed to get to the United States.

It was a well-planned coup. Representatives of the most distinguished sector of the Cuban oligarchy arrived in the Sierra "in defense of freedom," signed a joint declaration with the guerrilla chief isolated in the wilds of the Sierra, and returned with full freedom to play their trump card in Miami. But they overlooked one most important point.

Political coups always are limited by the opponents' strength, in this case, the weapons in the hands of the people. Quick action by our Chief, who had full confidence in the Guerrilla Army, averted the development of the treacherous plot. Months later, when the outcome of the Miami pact[17] became known, Fidel's fiery reply paralyzed the enemy. We were accused of being "divisionists" trying to impose our will from the remote regions of the Sierra, but the enemy had to change its strategy and look for a new trap, the Caracas pact.[18]

Our manifesto, dated July 12, 1957, was published in the newspapers. To us, the declaration was simply a short rest period on our march forward. Our main task, to defeat the enemy army in the battlefield, must go on. A new column was being organized with me as captain, and there were other promotions. Ramiro Valdés was promoted to captain and his platoon joined my column. Ciro Redondo, too, was to lead a platoon. The column included three platoons: the first platoon, the advance guard, was led by Lalo Sardiñas, who was also the detachment's Second-in-Command. Ramiro Valdés and Ciro led the other two. The column included almost 75 men, heterogeneously dressed and armed; however I was very proud of them. A few nights later, I was to feel even prouder, closer to the Revolution, anxious to prove that my officers' insignia were well deserved.

We wrote a letter of greeting and appreciation to "Carlos," Frank País' underground name, which was signed by all the officers of the Guerrilla Army who were able to write. Many of the Sierra peasants did not know how to read or write but they were an important part of our column. The signatures appeared on one column and the next column showed the signer's rank. When my turn came, Fidel simply said, "Make it Major." Thus, in a most informal manner, I was promoted to Major of the Second Column of the Guerrilla Army, later known as Column Four.

The letter, written while resting in a peasant's house, was the guerrilla fighters' warm message to their brother in the city, thanking him for his endless struggle to obtain supplies for us and lessen the enemy's pressure upon us.

There is a tinge of vanity hiding somewhere within each of us, and I was no exception. I was the proudest man in the world when I was promoted to Major. My insignia, a small star, was given to me by Celia. The award was accompanied by a gift, a wristwatch purchased in Santiago. My first mission was to set a trap for Sánchez Mosquera, but he was the smartest of all Batista's henchmen and had left the zone.

Something had to be done to justify the semi-independent life we were to lead in what was to be our new zone, so we began to plan a series of great deeds.

It was imperative that we celebrate the glorious date of July 26 and Fidel gave me free rein to do whatever I could, provided I took the necessary precautions. We had a new doctor with us, Sergio del Valle (now a Major in our Revolutionary Army). He, too, practised his profession within the limitations of the Sierra.

We had to prove that we were alive because we had received a few setbacks on the plains. Weapons that were to be used to open another front at Miranda sugar mill had been seized by the police, and several valuable leaders, among them Faustino Pérez, had been arrested. Fidel had opposed the division of forces but had given in to the pressure from the plains. The results were clear evidence of the correctness of his thinking and from then on we devoted ourselves to strengthening the Sierra Maestra as the base for the extension of the Guerrilla Army.

17

Attack on Bueycito

Several problems arose due to our independent life. Now it was necessary to establish a rigid discipline, organize the command and set up some sort of Staff to insure the success of coming battles. It was not an easy task since the new men lacked discipline.

No sooner was the detachment organized when a dear comrade, Lieutenant Maceo, left on a mission to Santiago. We never saw him again. He was killed in the city.

William Rodríguez, Raúl and Casero Mercader were promoted to lieutenant, in an effort to consolidate a small guerrilla force. One morning we heard the unpleasant news that a man called Wong "the Chinaman" had deserted, taking with him his 22-caliber rifle, a most valuable weapon under the circumstances. It was assumed he had returned to his home grounds in the foothills of the Sierra. Two men were sent after him but we lost all hope when Israel Pardo and Banderas returned after a fruitless search for other deserters. Taking into account Israel's strong physical condition and knowledge of the surrounding area, he was ordered to join my group for special missions.

We began to work out a very ambitious plan: to attack Estrada Palma first, at night, then continue to the nearby towns of Yara and Veguitas, seize the small army posts and return to the mountains. This would mean taking three enemy positions in one single attack, depending on the factor of surprise. We did some target practice, using ammunition sparingly, and found every weapon in good shape, with the exception of the Madzen machine-gun rifle that was old and dirty. We wrote Fidel asking whether or not he approved our plan. We received no answer from

Fidel, but on July 27 we heard the news on the radio: Raúl Castro, leading 200 men, had attacked Estrada Palma.

The magazine *Bohemia*, in the only uncensored issue of that time, published a special article describing the damage our troops had inflicted on Estrada Palma, where the army headquarters had been destroyed. The article mentioned Fidel Castro, Celia Sánchez and a myriad of revolutionaries who had come from the mountains. As usual, it was a mixture of truth and myth; the reporters never could figure out what had happened. The attack had been carried out by a small group led by Captain Guillermo García. Actually, there was no battle because Col. Barreras expected the 26th of July to be the date for strong attacks and had withdrawn his forces, not trusting his position. Actually, it was a sort of expedition that came to Estrada Palma. The next day, the army began the pursuit of our guerrillas and one of our men was caught asleep near San Lorenzo.

When we heard the news we made up our mind to move on and attack some other post on a date as close as possible to July 26, to maintain a state of affairs favorable to the insurrection.

On our way to La Maestra, near La Jeringa, we were met by one of the two men who had gone in search of the deserter. He said his comrade had told him that he was a close friend of Wong's and could not betray him. Then he urged him to desert, declaring he was not returning to the guerrillas. Our comrade warned him to stop, and when the man kept going away, he shot him. I gathered my troop on a hill nearby and told them they were going to witness the outcome of an attempt at desertion. I explained why the crime was punishable by death, the only sentence applicable to a betrayer of the Revolution. We marched by the body of the dead man, single file. Many of our new comrades were shaken by the sight of death, of a man, to boot, who had attempted to leave his post. Perhaps many were moved more by a certain affection for the man, together with a political weakness (understandable at that time), than by a feeling of disloyalty to the Revolution. These were hard times, and the shooting of the man was considered a lesson. It would be meaningless to mention the names of the protagonists in this drama. Let us say simply that the deserter was a young man, a humble peasant of that very same zone.

We were now traveling over familiar territory. On July 30, Lalo Sardiñas contacted an old friend, Armando Oliver, one of the zone's merchants. We set a rendezvous in a house in the California zone and there we met the merchant and Jorge Abich. We told Abich of our intention to attack Minas and Bueycito. We were risking a great deal by confiding in these people, but Lalo had full confidence in them.

Armando reported that Casillas visited this area on Sundays. Following the habitual custom of all army officers, he had a girl friend there. However, we were more inclined to mount a quick attack, based on surprise, rather than trust to luck and try to capture this notorious officer. The night of July 31 was set for the attack. Armando Oliver was to get trucks, guides and a sapper whose job was to blow up three bridges between the Bueycito and the Manzanillo-Bayamo roads. The following day at 2 P.M. we started our march toward the Maestra. It took two hours and once there we hid our knapsacks and went on. It was a long walk and on the way we passed a few houses. A party was going on in one of them and we stopped and gave the people a lecture, holding them responsible for any leaks about our whereabouts. Then we continued at full speed. Of course, in this case there was no great danger; there were no telephones or other means of communication in the Sierra. An informer would have to run fast to get ahead of us.

A comrade, Santiesteban, had a truck ready for us, together with two others that Oliver had sent. Sardiñas climbed aboard the first truck, Ramiro and I got on the second, Ciro and his group boarded the third, and we began the three-hour trip to the town of Las Minas. Army vigilance was focused almost entirely upon Las Minas, so it was our job to keep anyone from going to Bueycito. We left a rear guard, headed by Vilo Acuña, and went on to the outskirts of Bueycito.

At the entrance to town we stopped a coal truck and sent it ahead with one of our men to check up on the sentries. We knew that sometimes the army would set up a post and search everybody going in or out. This time there was no sentry. Every soldier was peacefully asleep.

Our plan was simple, although a little pretentious. Lalo Sardiñas was to attack the west side of the post, Ramiro would encircle it, and Ciro was to attack the front, using the Staff's machine gun. Oliver was to arrive in an automobile and turn his headlights on the guards, then Ramiro was to break in and capture everybody. Guards sleeping at home would be taken by surprise. Lieutenant Noda's squad kept their eyes open for any road traffic prior to the attack, and William was sent to blow up the bridge connecting Bueycito with the Central highway.

The plan never materialized. It was too much for a group of men unfamiliar with their surroundings and lacking experience. Ramiro lost some of his men in the dark, arrived late, and the automobile never came. There was a tense moment when we were placing our men and the dogs began to bark furiously.

I was walking along the town's main street when a man came out of a house. I gave him the order to halt and, taking me for one of his, he replied, "Rural Guard." When I pointed my gun at him, he jumped into the house and I could hear furniture and glass flying around inside. He escaped through the back of the house. I suppose it was a sort of silent agreement between us: I did not want to raise an alarm by firing, and, in turn, he did not warn his friends.

We were still looking for favorable positions when the sentry came out, puzzled by the barking of the dogs and perhaps by the noise made by my unexpected meeting with the soldier. I came face to face with the sentry. I was ready with my Thompson and he was carrying a Garand rifle. Israel Pardo was standing next to me. I gave the man the order to stop and he made a slight move. For me, that was more than enough. I pressed the trigger and nothing happened. Israel tried to fire his 22-caliber rifle and it jammed. I cannot imagine how Israel escaped unhurt. All I remember is running like a madman under the rain of bullets from the soldier's Garand. I turned a corner and stopped to get my gun back into firing condition. The soldier had inadvertently given the signal to start the attack, since his shots were the first heard that night. When the fire became general, the soldier hid behind a column, where we found him when the attack ended. It had taken only a few minutes.

While Israel went on to make contact, the shooting ended and we received the surrender. Ramiro's men had attacked the building as soon as they heard the first shots. They had riddled a door leading to the back of the building.

We found 12 soldiers, six of whom were wounded. We had lost one man, Pedro Rivero, a newcomer to our ranks, who was shot in the chest. Three others were slightly wounded. Once we had removed everything that was useful to us, we set the building on fire and boarded the trucks. We had captured the sergeant and an informer named Orán.

It was already daylight and everybody in town was offering us beer and cold drinks. The bridge to the highway had been blown up and we blew up another small bridge over a stream. The sapper came back with Oliver and he remained with us as a full-fledged member. He was a priceless acquisition. His name is Cristino Naranjo, who became a Major and was murdered by counter-revolutionaries after the triumph of the Revolution.

Our group came to Las Minas, where we stopped and held a little meeting. Playing his role to the hilt, one of the Abiches, a storekeeper, asked us in the name of the people to release the sergeant and the informer. We replied that we kept them as prisoners to safeguard the lives of the inhabitants, but as long as the people insisted, we would agree. Thus, we settled two things: the prisoners were released and the townspeople were safe. On the way to the Sierra we buried our comrade in the town's cemetery. Very few recognizance planes were flying over us at the time, so we stopped at a grocery store to take care of the wounded. One man had been shot in the shoulder, a surface wound, but it had torn the flesh away, making the treatment somewhat difficult; another was hit in the hand by a small caliber bullet. The third had a tremendous bump on his head. It seems that the army mules became frightened during the battle and began to kick right and left. One of the kicks landed on the wall and a piece of plaster landed on our comrade's head.

At Altos de California, we left the trucks and distributed the arms. Although my participation in the battle had been insignificant and none too heroic, since I had presented my posterior to the few shots fired in my direction, I took a Browning machine-gun rifle, the best one in the post. I threw away the Thompson and its unpredictable ammunition. The best fighters were given the best arms, and those who had performed worst were given leave of absence. These included the "wets," a group of men who had fallen into the river when they had tried to escape at the beginning of the battle. Among the best fighters, we can mention Captain Ramiro Valdés, who led the attack, and Raúl Castro Mercader, who played a decisive role in the short battle.

Back in the hills, we heard about the state of siege and the censorship. We also heard the terrible news of Frank País death. Frank had been murdered in the streets of Santiago, an enormous loss to the Revolution. It was the end of one of the purest, most brilliant figures of the Cuban Revolution.

The people of Santiago and Havana, in fact the entire population of Cuba, went into the spontaneous August strike,[19] the government's partial censorship became complete, and we entered a new stage, marked by absolute silence on the part of the pseudo-oppositionists on one hand, and by savage murders committed by Batista's henchmen all over the island, on the other. This time, the people of Cuba were ready for war.

When Frank País was murdered, we lost one of our most valuable fighters, but the people's reaction to the crime showed that additional forces were joining the struggle and the people's fighting spirit had grown.

18

Battle of El Hombrito

The column had been organized less than a month before, and already we had begun our sedentary life in the Sierra. We had camped in the valley of El Hombrito, the "Little Man," so named because two superimposed rocks on the summit of the Sierra resembled the figure of a small person.

Ours was a troop of new recruits, and the men had to be trained before they undertook difficult tasks, and yet we had to be ready for battle at any moment. It was our duty to attack any enemy units that dared invade what was already the "free territory of Cuba," that is, a certain section of the Sierra Maestra.

On the night of August 29, a peasant reported a large body of soldiers headed for the Sierra over El Hombrito road leading to the valley. We were very skeptical about such reports, so I told the man that he would be subjected to all sorts of punishment if he happened to be lying, but he kept swearing that it was all true, that the soldiers were now at the farm of Julio Zapatero, less than two miles from the Sierra.

That night we got into position. Lalo Sardiñas' platoon was hidden among ferns, and their duty was to hit the enemy as soon as they were stopped. Ramiro Valdés and his men, with less firepower, were to begin an "acoustic" attack to start the alarm. Although not powerfully armed, they were in a less dangerous position as the enemy had to cross a deep ravine to get close to them.

The trail the enemy had to enter was on the edge of the hill where Lalo lay in ambush. Ciro was to carry out an oblique attack and I, with the best-armed men, was to open hostilities. The best squad was Mercader's, so they were positioned as shock-troops to reap the fruits of victory. Our plan was simple. When the enemy reached a curve on the trail, making an almost 90° turn around a rock, I was to let 10 or 12 men go by, then open fire upon the last one, to separate the vanguard from the rest of the column, while the sharpshooters would take care of the men that had been cut off. Raúl Mercader's squad would take the dead soldiers' weapons, and we would all withdraw, covered by the rear guard under Lieutenant Vilo Acuña.

At dawn, from Ramiro Valdés' position, we noticed activity around Zapatero's house. A few men were walking in and out, putting on their helmets. We knew that the peasant had been telling the truth. We were all ready for action.

I took my position, as we kept our eyes on the enemy soldiers who were beginning their slow climb. I waited for what seemed an interminable period of time, my finger on the trigger of the Browning rifle, ready for battle. We could hear their voices and shouts as they marched on, not suspecting an ambush. The first man went by, then the second. They were so far apart from each other I began to think there would be no time to wait for 12 to pass. As I counted six, I heard a shout and one of the soldiers raised his head in a gesture of surprise. I opened fire, hitting the sixth man. The fire became general, and at the second burst of automatic rifle the men disappeared from the trail. I told Mercader's squad to attack, while a few volunteers joined the attack on the same spot; now we had opened fire from both sides. Lieutenant Orestes and Mercader were on their way in, and other men, protected by a rock, concentrated their fire on the enemy column that was part of a company commanded by Major Sosa. Rodolfo Vázquez took the weapon away from the man I had wounded. Unfortunately, he was only a medical corpsman whose entire equipment consisted of a 45-caliber revolver and a few shells. The other five men had thrown themselves down a ravine, escaping along the bottom of a dry stream. Soon, we heard the first bazookas fired by the enemy, now recovered from the unexpected attack.

A Maxim machine gun and my rifle were our only heavy-caliber weapons, but the Maxim would not work and Julio Pérez could do nothing with it.

On Ramiro's side, Israel and Joel Iglesias, armed with their puny weapons, had advanced toward the enemy. Shot-guns went off everywhere, adding to the soldiers' confusion. I ordered the two lateral platoons to retreat, then followed them, leaving the rear guard to provide cover until Lalo Sardiñas' platoon withdrew. We had already planned a second line of resistance.

Vilo Acuña caught up with us and told of Hermes Leyva's death. We came face to face with a platoon sent by Fidel, whom I had warned about the imminent battle with superior forces. Ignacio Pérez was at the head of this platoon. Retreating about 1,000 yards, we set up our new ambush. The soldiers came to the plateau where the attack had taken place and we watched as they burned the body of Hermes Leyva, in a savage act of revenge. In our impotent fury, all we could do was to fire our rifles and they returned our fire with their bazookas.

I discovered that the shout which provoked my hurried shot was a remark made by one of the soldiers. He had shouted something like "this is a picnic!"—probably indicating that he was getting close to the summit. The attack proved our lack of combat training, since we had been unable to fire accurately at an enemy no more than 20 yards away. Even so, it was a big victory for us. We had managed to stop Merob Sosa's column, and they had now withdrawn. We also obtained one small weapon, but at a very high price, the life of one of our comrades. We accomplished this with inefficient arms, against a complete company of at least 140 men, well equipped for modern war, who had launched heavy bazooka fire, perhaps even mortars, against us, although their attack had been just as haphazard as ours.

After the battle, a few men were promoted, among them Alfonso Zayas, who was made a lieutenant. Next day, we talked with Fidel, who was very happy with the results of an attack he had launched against the soldiers in Las Cuevas. Some of our comrades had been killed: Juventino Alarcón of Manzanillo, one of the first to join our guerrillas; Pastor, Yayo, Castillo, and Oliva, a great fighter and a fine boy, whose father was a lieutenant in Batista's army.

Fidel's attack had been quite important since it was not an ambush but an actual assault on a camp which was fairly well defended. The enemy had suffered many losses and had abandoned their position the following day. One of the heroes had been Pilón, the "Negro," a great fighter. They told us Pilón had come to a hut where he saw a row of strange-looking lengths of pipe next to a number of small boxes. They were bazookas, but neither Pilón nor any of us had even seen one at close range. Pilón was wounded in the leg and had to abandon the hut, and we lost a great opportunity to get our hands on these weapons, so valuable against small fortifications.

Our battle had new repercussions. A few days later, an army dispatch announced five or six dead. In addition to burning our comrade's body, the soldiers had murdered five or six peasants whom Merob Sosa suspected of having reported to us about the army's whereabouts. Those poor peasants were murdered and their houses were set afire. I remember the names of Abigail, Calixto, Pablito Lebón—of Haitian descent—and Gonzalo González, all far removed, or at least partly removed, from our struggle. They knew about our cause, they suspected we were in the zone, but they were completely innocent of our ambush. We knew very well the methods used by Batista's officers to obtain information and we kept our moves secret. In case a peasant happened to go by an ambush we kept him with us until the attack was over.

The battle proved that it was easy, under the circumstances, to attack enemy columns on the march. We realized the advantage of firing upon the head of the column and of trying to kill the leading men, immobilizing the rest of them. We continued this practice until it became an established system, so efficient that the soldiers stopped coming to the Sierra Maestra and refused to be part of the advance guard. Of course, it took more than one battle for our system to materialize. At the time, we were satisfied to analyze our small victories together with Fidel. They were indeed victories, these battles between a well equipped army and our poorly prepared soldiers.

This was more or less the moment when the soldiers abandoned the Sierra. The only man who ever came back, in a show of audacity, was Sánchez Mosquera, the bravest as well as the most notorious murderer and thief among Batista's military officers.

19

"El Patojo"

A few days ago, the news from Guatemala reported the deaths of several patriots, among them Julio Roberto Cáceres Valle.

In our profession as revolutionaries, amidst the class struggle shaking the entire Continent, we find that death is a frequent accident. But the death of a friend, who was our comrade during difficult moments as well as during many moments of hopeful dreaming, is always painful. Julio Roberto was a great friend. He was small and rather weak physically, so we nicknamed him "El Patajo," which in Guatemalan slang means "little one" or "child."

While in Mexico, El Patojo had witnessed the birth of the idea of a Revolution. He had offered his services as a volunteer, but Fidel did not want to involve foreigners in this project of national liberation in which I had the honor to participate.

Shortly after the triumph of the Revolution, El Patojo sold his few belongings and came to me. He occupied several positions in public administration and became Chief of Personnel of the Industry Department of INRA (National Institute of Agrarian Reform), but he was never too happy with his jobs. He was looking for something else, his country's liberation. Like all of us, he had undergone a deep transformation. He had changed from a bewildered boy who had left his country without fully understanding the reason for defeat, into the fully conscious revolutionary that he now was.

The first time I saw El Patojo was aboard a train. We were running away from Guatemala following Arbenz' overthrow. Our destination was Tapachula, then Mexico City. He was much younger than I, but we soon became close friends. Together we made the trip from Chiapas to Mexico City, facing the same problems. We were poor and beaten, and we had to make a living amidst indifferent, if not hostile, surroundings.

El Patojo was completely broke and I had only a few pesos. I purchased a camera and we became clandestine photographers, taking pictures of people visiting parks, etc. Our partner was a Mexican who owned the laboratory where we developed and printed our photographs. We became thoroughly familiar with Mexico City, walking from one end to the other, delivering our miserable photos and struggling with our customers in an effort to convince them that the little child in the print really looked beautiful and that the price of one Mexican peso for such a work of art was a tremendous bargain. We practised our profession for several months and managed to eat quite regularly. Gradually, we fared a little better, until the adventures of a revolutionary life separated us. I have already explained that Fidel did not want our small army to be a mosaic of nationalities.

El Patojo continued his life as a newspaperman, studying physics at the University of Mexico, cutting short his studies, going back to the University, without getting ahead. He made his living working at various occupations, never asking for anything. To this day, I cannot say whether that sensitive boy was too timid or too proud to recognize his weaknesses and personal problems and to approach some friend and ask for help. El Patojo was an introvert, a man of great intelligence, well educated, and endowed with tremendous sensitivity which, toward the end, he devoted to serving his people. Already a Party man, he belonged to the Guatemalan Workers' Party, he had acquired great discipline and he was a good prospect as a revolutionary cadre. There was very little left of his former touchiness and proud demeanor. The Revolution cleanses men, improving and developing them, as the farmer corrects the defects on a plant and brings out its best qualities.

In Cuba, El Patojo and I shared the same house, as becomes old friends, but the old mutual confidence no longer existed. On a few occasions, I suspected what El Patojo was after. I had seen him hard at work, studying one of his country's native languages. One day, he came to me and said he was leaving, that the time had come for him to do his duty.

El Patojo had no military training. He simply felt that it was his duty to return to his country and fight, weapon in hand, in an attempt to imitate our guerrilla warfare. We held a long conversation, rare at the time. I limited my recommendations to three points: constant mobility, constant mistrust, and constant vigilance. Mobility: never stay in the same place, never stay more than two nights in the same spot, never stop moving from one place to another. Mistrust: at the beginning, do not trust your own shadow, never trust friendly peasants, informers, guides, or contact men. Do not trust anything or anybody until a zone is completely liberated. Vigilance: constant guard and scouting, setting up camp in a safe spot, and above all, never sleep with a roof over your head, never sleep in a house that can be surrounded. It was a synthesis of our guerrilla experience, the only thing I could give my friend. Could I tell him not to do it? By what right? We had tried something when it was considered impossible, and now he was convinced that it was possible.

El Patojo departed, and a short time later we heard about his death. As always in these cases, we hoped that there had been some mistake, perhaps a mix-up in names. Unfortunately, it was true; his own mother had identified the body. Others, too, had been killed—a group of his comrades, perhaps as intelligent and self-sacrificing as El Patojo, but unknown to us.

Once again there is the bitter taste of defeat. The question left unanswered: Why not profit by the experience of others? Why weren't these simple instructions obeyed? Every effort was made to learn exactly how El Patojo had died. The exact facts are still unknown, but one could say that the zone was badly chosen, the men's physical condition was below par, they were too trusting, and above all, there was not enough vigilance. The repressive army came upon them by surprise, killing a few; the men were dispersed and the soldiers caught up with them once again. Some were captured and others, like El Patojo, were killed in the battle. Once the guerrillas lost cohesion, the rest was probably an open manhunt, similar to what happened to us at Alegría de Pío.

Once again, young blood has been spilled on American soil, in the struggle for liberty. Another battle has been lost.

Let us take time off to cry over the fallen comrades while we continue to sharpen our machetes. Based on the unfortunate as well as valuable experience of our beloved dead, let us adopt the firm resolution not to repeat mistakes, and to avenge the death of every one of them by winning battles and attaining liberation.

At the time of his departure, El Patojo made no recommendations; he mentioned no one. He had no personal belongings to be concerned about. However, mutual friends in Mexico brought me some verses he had written in a simple notebook. They are a revolutionary's last verses. They are also a song of love to the Revolution, to the motherland, and to a woman.

The final injunction in these verses appears to be directed to the woman whom El Patojo met and loved, here in Cuba.

> *Take it, it is only a heart*
> *hold it in your hand*
> *and at daybreak,*
> *open your hand*
> *and let the sun's rays warm it . . .*

El Patojo's heart has remained with us, waiting for the lover's hand, the loving hands of an entire people, to allow the sun to warm it on the dawn of a new day that will shine for Guatemala and all America. Today, there is a small School of Statistics named "Julio Roberto Cáceres Valle" at the Ministry of Industry, where El Patojo left numerous friends. Later, when freedom comes to Guatemala, his beloved name must appear on a school, a factory or a hospital, anywhere people struggle and work in the construction of the new society.

20

Camilo[20]

Memory is a way of reviving the past, the dead. To remember Camilo is to remember things which are past or dead, and yet Camilo Cienfuegos is a living part of the Cuban Revolution, immortal by his very nature. I would like simply to give our comrades of the Rebel Army an idea of who this invincible guerrilla fighter was. I am able to do so, since, from the sad hours of the first setback at Alegría de Pío, we were always together. And it is my duty to do so, because, far more than a comrade in arms, in joys and victories, Camilo was a real brother.

I never got to know him in Mexico, as he joined us at the last minute. He had come from the United States without any previous recommendation, and we in those risky days had no confidence in him, nor indeed in anyone else. He came on the *Granma,* simply one among the 82 who crossed the sea at the mercy of the elements to carry out a feat that was to shake the entire continent. I realized what he was like before I actually got to know him when I heard a characteristic exclamation of his during the disastrous battle of Alegría de Pío. I was wounded, stretched out in a clearing next to a comrade covered with blood who was firing his last rounds, ready to die fighting. I heard someone cry weakly: "We're lost. Let's surrender." And a clear voice from somewhere among the men shouted in reply: "Nobody surrenders here!"—followed by a four-letter word.

The battle ended, we survived, and I went on breathing, thanks to the help of Comrade Almeida. Five of us wandered around the steep cliffs near Cabo Cruz. One clear, moonlit night we came upon three other comrades sleeping peacefully, without any fear of the soldiers. We jumped them, believing them to be enemies. Nothing happened, but the incident served later as the occasion for a mutual joke between us—the fact that I was among those who had caught them by surprise, and the fact that it was I who had to raise the white flag so that they would not shoot us, mistaking us for Batista's soldiers.

And so then there were eight of us. Camilo was hungry and wanted to eat; he didn't care what or where, he simply wanted to eat. This led to some serious disagreements with him, because he constantly wanted to approach peasants' huts to ask for food. Twice, for having followed the advice of "the hungry ones," we nearly fell into the hands of enemy soldiers who had killed dozens of our comrades. On the ninth day "the hungry ones" won out, and we approached a hut, ate, and all got sick. And among the sickest, naturally, was Camilo who, like a hungry lion, had gulped down an entire kid.

During that period I was more a medic than a soldier. I put Camilo on a special diet and ordered him to stay behind in the hut, where he would receive proper attention. That trouble passed, and we were together again, and the days lengthened into weeks and months during which many comrades were killed. Camilo showed his mettle, earning the rank of lieutenant of the vanguard of our one and only beloved Column, which would later be called the José Martí Column One, under Fidel's personal command. Almeida and Raúl were captains; Camilo, lieutenant of the vanguard; Efigenio Ameijeiras, leader of the rear guard; Ramiro Valdés, lieutenant in one of Raúl's platoons; and Calixto, soldier in another platoon. In other words, all our forces were born there, where I was the group's lieutenant medic. Later, following the battle of El Uvero, I was given the rank of captain, and, a few days later, the rank of major and the command of a column.

One day Camilo was made captain of the column which I commanded, Column Four. We bore that number to deceive the enemy, as actually there were only two. And it was there that Camilo began his career of exploits, and it was with untiring effort and extraordinary zeal that, time and again, he hunted down enemy soldiers. Once he shot an enemy scout at such close range that he caught the man's rifle before it hit the ground. Another time he planned to let the first of the enemy soldiers go by until they were abreast of our troop, and then open flank fire. The ambush never came off because someone in our group got nervous and opened fire before the enemy got close enough. By then Camilo was Camilo, "Lord of the Vanguard," a real guerrilla fighter who was able to assert himself in his own colorful way of fighting.

I recall my anxiety during the second attack on Pino del Agua, when Fidel ordered me to stay with him and gave Camilo the responsibilty of attacking one of the enemy's flanks. The idea was simple. Camilo was to attack and take one end of the enemy camp and then surround it. The firing started, and he and his men took the sentry post and continued advancing, entering the settlement, killing or taking prisoner every soldier in their path. The town was taken house by house until finally the enemy organized resistance and the barrage of bullets began to take its toll among our ranks. Valuable comrades, among them Noda and Capote, lost their lives in this battle.

An enemy machine-gunner advanced, surrounded by his men, but soon he found himself amidst a veritable storm of gunfire. The machine-gunner's assistants were killed, and the soldier manning the gun dropped it and fled. It was dawn. The attack had begun at night. Camilo hurled himself across the machine gun to seize it and defend it, and was shot twice. A bullet pierced his left thigh, and another hit him in the abdomen. He got away, and his comrades carried him. We were almost two miles away, with the enemy between us. We could hear machine-gun bursts and shouting: "There goes Camilo's gun!" "That's Camilo firing!" and then *vivas* for Batista. We all thought that Camilo had been killed. Later we praised his luck that the bullet had entered and left his abdomen without hitting his intestines or any vital organ.

Then came the tragic day of April 9,[21] and Camilo, the trailblazer, went to the Oriente plains and became a legend, striking terror into the hearts of the enemy forces mobilized in the Bayamo area. Once he was surrounded by 600 men, and there were only 20 in the rebel force. They resisted an entire day against an enemy advance that included two tanks, and at night they made a spectacular escape.

Later came the offensive, and in the face of imminent danger and the concentration of forces Camilo was called, as he was the man Fidel trusted to leave in his place when he went to a specific front. Then came the marvelous epic of the invasion and his chain of victories on the plains of Las Villas[22]—a difficult feat, as the terrain afforded little natural protection. These actions were magnificent for their audacity, and at the same time one could already see Camilo's political attitude, his decision regarding political problems, his strength and his faith in the people.

Camilo was happy, down-to-earth and a joker. I remember that in the Sierra a peasant, one of our great, magnificent, anonymous heroes, had been called a name by Camilo, at the same time making an ugly gesture. One day the peasant came to see me as head of the column, complaining that he shouldn't be insulted and that he was no "ventriloquist." As I didn't understand, I spoke to Camilo, asking him to explain the man's strange attitude. What happened was that Camilo had looked at the man with an air of disrespect and called him a ventriloquist, and, as the peasant didn't know what a ventriloquist was, he was terribly offended.

Camilo had a little alcohol burner, and he used to cook cats and offer them as a delicacy to new recruits who joined us. It was one of the many tests of the Sierra, and more than one failed this preliminary "examination" when he refused to eat the cat proffered. Camilo was a man of anecdotes, a million anecdotes. They were a part of his nature. His appreciation of people and his ability to get along with them were a part of his personality. These qualities, which today we sometimes forget or overlook, were present in all his actions, something precious that few men can attain. It is true, as Fidel has said, that he had no great amount of "book learning," but he had the natural intelligence of the people who had chosen him from among thousands to place in that privileged place earned by his audacity, his tenacity, his intelligence and devotion. Camilo was uncompromisingly loyal to two things, and with the same results: he had unlimited loyalty and devotion to Fidel and to the people. Fidel and the people march together, and Camilo's devotion was projected toward them both.

Who killed Camilo? Who killed the man who, in the lives of others like him, lives on in the people? Such men do not die so long as the people do not authorize it. The enemy killed him, killed him because they wanted him to die, because there are no completely safe airplanes, because pilots are not able to acquire all the necessary experience, because he was overloaded with work and had to be in Havana as quickly as possible. He was killed by his drive.[23] Camilo did not measure danger. He utilized it as a game, he played with it, he courted it, he attracted and handled it and, with his guerrilla's mentality, a mere cloud could not detain or deviate him from the line he was following. It happened at a time everyone knew him, admired and loved him; it could have happened before, and then his story would have been known only as that of a mere guerrilla captain.

There will be many Camilos, as Fidel has said; and there have been Camilos, I can add—Camilos who died before completing the magnificent cycle of work that he had achieved, thus entering the pages of history. Camilo and the other Camilos—the ones who fell early and those still to come—are the index of the people's strength; they are the most complete expression of the heights that can be reached by a nation fighting to defend its purest ideals and with complete faith in the fulfillment of its noblest goals.

There is too much to be said to allow me to put his essence into a lifeless mold, which would be equivalent to killing him. It is better to leave it like this, in general descriptive terms, without spelling out in black and white his socio-economic ideology, which was not precisely defined. But we must always bear in mind that there was never a man—not even before the Revolution—comparable to Camilo: a complete revolutionary, a man of the people, an artist of the Revolution, sprung from the heart of the Cuban nation. His mind was incapable of the slightest slackening or disappointment. He is an object of daily remembrance; he is one who did this or that, something by Camilo; he who left this exact and indelible imprint on the Cuban Revolution, who is present among those who fell early in their revolutionary careers and those heroes who are yet to come. In his constant and eternal rebirth, Camilo is the image of the people.

APPENDIX

FOUR ARTICLES ON THE
REVOLUTIONARY WAR

Written in July 1959. The present version is based on the articles as published in Granma, *English edition, October 22, 1967.*

1

Beginning of a Revolution

The history of the military aggression consummated on March 10, 1952, in the "bloodless coup" directed by Fulgencio Batista, does not begin, of course, the very day of the coup. Its antecedents must be sought far back in the history of Cuba, much before U.S. Ambassador Sumner Wells' intervention in 1933,[1] even before the Platt Amendment in 1901,[2] before the landing of the hero Narciso López,[3] special envoy of the U.S. annexationists, all the way back to its roots in the time of John Quincy Adams, who, at the beginning of the 18th century, announced the theme of his country's policy toward Cuba: an apple that, dropping from the Spanish tree, was predestined to fall into the hands of Uncle Sam. These are links in a long chain of continental aggression aimed not exclusively at Cuba.

This ebb and flow of the imperialist tide is marked now by the overthrow of democratic governments and then by the appearance of new governments as a result of the irresistible drive of the masses. History shows similar characteristics in all of Latin America. Dictatorial governments represent a small minority and come into power by means of *coups d'etat;* democratic governments with a broad popular base arise painfully and, before taking power, often are already stigmatized by a series of previous concessions which they were forced to make to stabilize their position in the first place. And though the Cuban Revolution is, in that sense, an exception in all America, it is necessary to point out the antecedents to this whole process. The author, carried to and fro by the tides of the social events shaking America, had an opportunity, as a result of these events, to meet another American exile, Fidel Castro.

I met him on one of those cold Mexican nights, and I

remember that our first conversation dealt with the subject of international policy. Within a few hours of our meeting in the early morning hours, I had already become one of his future revolutionaries. But I wish to explain how and why I met in Mexico the present chief of the Government of Cuba.

This happened in 1954 during the ebb-tide of democratic governments, when the last American revolutionary democracy still in power in this area—that of Jacobo Arbenz—fell as a result of the cold, premeditated aggression of the United States, hiding behind the smokescreen of its continental propaganda. Secretary of State Dulles was by a rare coincidence also stockholder and attorney of the United Fruit Company, the most powerful imperialist enterprise in Guatemala.

One left Guatemala. Then, defeated, united to the Guatemalan people by a bond of common sorrow, one waited, seeking a way to rebuild a future for that grief-stricken country, while Fidel had come to Mexico seeking a neutral ground where he could prepare his men for the great push. Internal dissension had already set in, after the assault on the Moncada garrison in Santiago de Cuba, resulting in the desertion of the weak-kneed, those who for one reason or another joined political parties or revolutionary groups expecting less sacrifice. The first new recruits already were joining the ranks of the newly-born 26th of July Movement, named for the date of the attack on the Moncada garrison in 1953.

A most difficult task awaited those responsible for the training of new recruits under conditions of unavoidable secrecy essential in Mexico. We had to contend with the Mexican Government, with agents of the FBI and of Batista, with all those forces which at times combined their efforts in various ways, in a situation where money and bribery played an important role. Moreover, we had to contend with the spies of Trujillo [the Dominican tyrant] and the poor selection of men, especially in Miami. Overcoming all these obstacles, we had to plan our departure, later our landing and the rest which, at the time, seemed easy to us. Today we are able to evaluate the cost in effort, sacrifice and lives.

Fidel Castro, assisted by a small team of trusted revolutionaries, devoted all his abilities and extraordinary working spirit to the task of organizing the armed forces that were to sail for Cuba. He seldom attended classes in military tactics, as he did not have enough time left for this. The rest of us were able to learn a good deal from General Alberto Bayo.[4] My almost immediate impression after attending the first few classes was that victory was possible, which I had doubted when I joined the rebel chief, to whom from the very beginning I was tied by a bond of romantic sympathy for adventure and the thought that it would be worthwhile to meet death on a foreign beach for so pure an ideal.

A few months went by. Our marksmanship improved, and sharpshooters emerged. We found a ranch in Mexico where, under the direction of General Bayo and with myself as chief of personnel, we made the final plans for departure in 1956. However, at that time two different Mexican units—both in Batista's pay—were hunting for Fidel Castro. One of them was lucky enough to arrest him, but committed the absurdity, to their loss, of not killing him after taking him prisoner. Many of Fidel's followers were captured a few days later. Our ranch on the outskirts of Mexico City fell into the hands of the police, and we all landed in jail.

This setback delayed the last part of the first stage. Some of us were in prison for 57 days with the threat of extradiction hanging over our heads. Major Calixto García and I are witnesses to this. However, at no time did we lose our personal confidence in Fidel Castro. We could almost say that Fidel's attitude of friendship at times jeopardized his position as a revolutionary. I recall that I specifically explained my situation to him: an alien, illegally residing in

Mexico, with many charges against me. I told him that on no account was the revolution to be stopped for my sake, that they could leave me behind, that I understood the situation and that I could join the struggle from whatever place I was ordered to do so. The only effort to be made, I requested, was to have me sent to a nearby country and not to Argentina. I also recall Fidel's firm reply: "I will not forsake you." As a result, it was necessary to spend precious time and money to get us out of the Mexican jail. Such personal gestures by Fidel toward those he loves are the key to the strong devotion created around him, where a feeling of loyalty based on principle is added to a loyalty based on friendship, making the Cuban Rebel Army an indivisible whole.

The days went by as we worked in secrecy, hiding where we could, avoiding appearing in public as much as possible, seldom going out on the streets.

2

The *Granma* Landing

A few months later we learned there was a traitor among us whose identity was still unknown. He had sold the enemy one lot of weapons. We also learned he had sold the yacht and a radio transmitter, although the "bill of sale" had not yet been made out. This first delivery served to prove to Cuban authorities that the traitor did, indeed, know our organization from within. His delivery of the weapons also saved us by tipping us off. From that moment, we had to proceed with feverish haste. The yacht *Granma* was readied at full speed. We gathered together all supplies we could get hold of, which were few indeed, as well as uniforms, rifles, equipment and two anti-tank rifles with practically no ammunition for them. Finally, on November

25, 1956, at 2 A.M., Fidel's words, treated as a joke by the
official press, began to turn into reality: "In the year 1956,
we will be free men or martyrs."

We sailed from the port of Tuxpán with all lights out,
with an infernal overcrowding of all sorts of supplies and
men. The weather was bad, but though navigation was
prohibited, the waters of the estuary were calm. We crossed
the entrance into the Gulf in the region of Yucatán and, a
few moments later, turned on the ship's lights. Then began
a frantic search for our antihistamine tablets against seasickness, which we could not locate. We sang the Cuban
National Anthem and the 26th of July Anthem for perhaps
five minutes, after which the situation on the entire ship
assumed a ridiculously tragic aspect. Men seized by an
attack of seasickness held their stomachs, while their faces
reflected their anguish. Some buried their heads in buckets
while others were lying about, motionless, their clothes
covered with vomit. With the exception of two or three
experienced seamen and four or five others, all the 83 men
aboard were victims of seasickness. After the fourth or fifth
day, the general situation improved somewhat. We discovered that what we thought was a leak was only an open
faucet in the men's room, but by then we had already
jettisoned all surplus weight to lighten the ship's load.

The route chosen included a wide sweep around the
south coast of Cuba, skirting Jamaica and the island of
Grand Cayman, to a spot near the town of Niquero in the
province of Oriente. We were rather behind our time
schedule. On the 30th, we heard via radio the news of the
Santiago de Cuba riots organized by our comrade, Frank
País, which were to coincide with our landing in Cuba. The
following night, December 1, we made straight for the
Cuban coast, searching frantically for the Cabo Cruz Light.
We were running low on water, fuel and food. At 2 A.M., on
a stormy, dark night, the situation was disquieting. Look-
outs went to and fro searching for the beam of light, which
could not be seen on the horizon. Roque, a former lieutenant

in the Cuban Navy, climbing once more to the top bridge trying to make out the Cabo Cruz Light, tripped and fell overboard. Shortly after, starting again on our way, we finally saw the light, but the slow speed of the vessel made the last few hours of sailing seem endless. It was daylight when we landed in Cuba in the vicinity of Belic, on Playa de las Coloradas.

We had been spotted by a coastal vessel which telegraphed our position to Batista's army. Leaving the yacht as hastily and with as little equipment as possible, scarcely had we entered the swamp when Batista's airplanes began to attack. Marching through swamps, under cover of the mangroves, we could not be spotted and harassed by the planes, but the army of the dictatorship was already at our heels.

We spent several hours getting out of the swamp in which we had landed, thanks to our lack of knowledge of the area and the irresponsibility of a comrade who had claimed to know it. We reached solid ground, lost, stumbling along like so many shadows or ghosts marching in response to some obscure psychic impulse. We had been through seven days of constant hunger and seasickness during the sea crossing, topped by three still more terrible days on land. Exactly ten days after our departure from Mexico, during the early morning hours of December 5, following a night-long march interrupted by faintings and frequent rest periods, we reached a spot paradoxically known as Alegría de Pío.[5] It was a small wooded area, bordered on one side by a canefield and on the remaining sides by valleys leading to thick woods in the distance. It was an ill-suited place to camp, but we called a halt to spend the day there, planning to continue on our march the following night.

At four o'clock that afternoon, without the slightest warning and to our complete surprise, we heard the first shot, followed by a symphony of lead over our heads. We were not as yet accustomed to such virile sport. One of our comrades fell and I personally felt the unpleasant sensation in my flesh of simultaneous baptism by fire and blood. We got out of there as best we could, every man for himself or in groups, not heeding our leader's orders, lacking contact with our captains, and in a state of complete confusion. I remember the push Major Almeida gave me, lacking the will to walk, and it was thanks only to his imperious orders that I got up and kept going, believing all the time that I was near death. In a kaleidoscopic scene, men ran by shouting, the wounded called for help, some tried to take cover behind slender stalks of sugar cane as if they were tree trunks, while, amidst the roar of battle, others signaled in terror for silence by placing a finger over their lips. Suddenly, we heard the ominous cry, "The canefield is on fire!"

With Almeida in the lead, we made it through a lane between the thick woods. We pushed on until stopped by darkness and the trees, which prevented us from seeing the stars, still not far from the scene of our encounter with the army. We slept piled against one another. Everything was lost except our weapons and two canteens carried by Almeida and me. In this state, we went on for nine interminable days of suffering, without tasting cooked food, and chewing grass or raw corn. Some of the more valiant, including Camilo Cienfuegos, ate raw crabs.

During those nine days our morale crumbled. Throwing all caution to the wind, we approached a countryman's hut in search of food. There some of our men collapsed. News was both bad and encouraging. Together with reports of crimes supposedly committed by us, came the light of hope: Fidel was alive. Hair-raising accounts by the peasants prompted us to cache our rifles and try to cross a heavily-guarded highway armed with our pistols only. As a result, the weapons left in the care of the peasants were lost while we made our way toward the Sierra Maestra, where Fidel was.

Approximately 15 days after the disastrous landing, those of the 82 "castaways" of the *Granma*—as Comrade Juan

Manuel Márquez has described us—who were still in fighting condition were reunited. There were some 17 of us. Our list of casualties was long and depressing: Juan Manuel Márquez himself; "Ñico" López, a great comrade from the working class; Juan Smith, captain of our vanguard; and Cándido González, Fidel's aide, a revolutionary with a spotless record. It was a long list, to which new names were constantly being added, fulfilling Fidel's prediction: "In the year 1956 we will be free men or martyrs." Now we who were left, led by Fidel Castro, had the responsibility of raising high the banner of insurrection and turning the first part of that prediction—"we will be free men"—into reality, in honor of the martyrs who fell there as well as those who were dying day by day throughout Cuba, suffering torture or being murdered ruthlessly in an incredible holocaust of blood. It was equally incredible that this small group of men, still scarcely well-acquainted with one another, already spoke of victory, of taking the offensive.

All of us became aware of the unreserved affection felt for us by the peasants of the zone. They took care of us and, through a long chain of clandestine contacts, brought us to our prearranged meeting place, the house of Crescencio Pérez's brother. But the one who had the greatest faith in the people, who at all times showed his extraordinary powers of leadership, was Fidel. Already during those nights, those long nights—since our activities ceased at nightfall—sitting under the trees anywhere, we began to draw plan after plan for the present, for the near future and for victory. Those were happy hours, during which, as projects for the future followed one another rapidly, I acquired a taste for my first cigars (which I learned to smoke to drive away the overly-aggressive mosquitoes, until I was captured by the fragrance of the Cuban leaf).

The days passed and, little by little, new recruits came in. The first peasants started joining us, some unarmed, some with weapons that had been left by our comrades in the homes of friendly people or abandoned in canefields as they fled. Our small troop had 22 rifles at the time we stormed La Plata on January 17, 1957—45 days after our landing. That action gave Cuba fresh hope on learning of new encounters in the heart of the Sierra Maestra, though the operation was no more than a skirmish. We had caught by surprise an Army post of 12 to 15 men, who surrendered after an hour of fighting. In those moments, an hour of fighting was an hour of tremendous suffering. Fidel and I, who were expert marksmen with rifles equipped with telescopic sights, had 70 rounds each. Those with automatic rifles had 25 cartridges apiece; those with bolt-action guns, 15 each; while some of the machine-gunners had 20 to 30 each. We took the small Army post of La Plata with those weapons.

Five days later, with a dozen new rifles obtained from that action, we were able to defeat the advance guard of a detachment sent after us, commanded by Sánchez Mosquera, a figure of sinister reputation. This was followed by an impasse caused by a traitor within our ranks; he betrayed our position to the enemy who very nearly liquidated us on three different occasions. It is worth mentioning that this man had been personally charged with the mission of killing Fidel. One night he and Fidel slept under the same blanket. The traitor had a pistol, but could not gather enough courage to commit the murder, preferring to take the easier way of leaving our camp under various pretexts and guiding the enemy to our position. He was finally caught on his fourth try and executed. But the damage he had done was already great.

Herbert Matthews, a newsman from *The New York Times*, visited our camp in those days. He gave a full account to the world—and especially Cuba—of our existence in the Sierra Maestra and the assurance that Fidel was alive. Nevertheless, our trials were far from over. Our dangerous life continued, high up on inaccessible mountains, completely surrounded by soldiers of the dictatorship, and we could not yet count on the unanimous support of the people.

Many peasants still fled before us, fearing reprisals taken by government forces every time they learned of any contact, no matter how casual, between the people of the zone and our group.

One month later, about the middle of March, we were joined by a handful of men sent by Frank País from Santiago de Cuba. The inclusion of these men gave our Revolution a new character.

3

The Revolution Advances

The weapons brought by the new recruits were in no way extraordinary, but they strengthened the column considerably. We then initiated the march through new regions; for the first time we climbed the Turquino, the highest mountain in Cuba, leaving signs of our passing, and we continued walking for long days together through the undergrowth of the Sierra Maestra until we came close to the sawmills of Pino del Agua and Babún.

Patiently we awaited the right opportunity, which presented itself on May 28, 1957, to take the military garrison of El Uvero, situated on the coast where the Sierra Maestra drops down almost perpendicular to the sea. This battle for El Uvero was the fiercest of the war; of 120-140 men that took part on both sides, some 40 were put out of action, which meant that the dead and wounded amounted to approximately thirty per cent of all the combatants. The political outcome of the battle was extraordinary, since it took place at one of the few moments—after the *Granma* invasion—when there was no press censorship in the island. All of Cuba spoke about El Uvero. Despite the weapons taken from the enemy, 50 guns and ammunition, we encountered serious difficulties. As doctor, I was in charge of seven wounded, and we had to hide them in some huts not far away from the place of combat.

The column continued its march toward the customary camping places, and we joined up again in the following months, with the wounded who were fit by then. After the reunion I was made Major of another group which we called, for tactical reasons, the Fourth Column. The Fourth Column—actually the Second—took its place alongside the First, headed by Fidel Castro. Afterward, being much less harassed by the enemy because of its lesser political importance, the Fourth Column was able to form bases for the first factories and more permanent camps, and to end our nomadic life. We executed some actions of little significance, but most important was the stabilization that was achieved with great difficulty, carrying the matériel from distant regions on our shoulders.

In this way we were able to install a shoe factory and a saddlery, an armory with an electric lathe, a tinshop and smithy for the purpose, among other things, of making small metal grenades to be fired from a gun, an invention of ours. The grenade was fired by a blank cartridge and dubbed "M-26." We also built schools, recreation areas and ovens, to bake bread. Later on, the Radio Rebelde transmitter was installed, and our first clandestine newspaper with the same name as the Mambi newspaper of the wars of 1863 and 1895,[6] El Cubano Libre, was published.

All these installations were at times in danger from the enemy, but the place chosen in La Mesa valley proved invulnerable to advancing troops and we were able to maintain the position safely until the end of the war.

Our forces increased constantly. We obtained weapons in victorious battles on one front or another. The second battle of Pino del Agua, a positive triumph for our men, also took place during a letup in press censorship and had great political repercussions. Our growth made possible the Second Eastern Front. At that time, in March 1958, Major Raúl Castro took command of the Frank País Sixth Column, named in honor of the veteran militant who fell in Santiago de Cuba. Crossing the Central Highway, Raúl buried himself in the hills of Mayarí, to the north of Oriente province.

Afterwards, this Second Eastern Front would have enormous importance in the development of the war. It was the best organized in all ways, having seven departments that functioned like real ministries, where justice was carried out, public works were organized, revolutionary laws for the army made, and transport established. Great advances were made in comparison with our modest task of the Sierra Maestra. It was a vigorous infant; the factories were built on an almost industrial scale, since abundant materials were at hand. We now had more money to work with, raised by taxes levied on big companies and sugar centrals.

Major Almeida was also transferred from the old haunt to a site close to Santiago de Cuba, creating another front with Column Three. There were now four columns in the Sierra Maestra, and fighting took place on one front or another with more or less intensity, but the whole of Oriente Province was up in arms. Small actions were then initiated in the region of the Escambray, in the center of the island, which had never been a source of concern to the regime until our arrival. Some uprisings also occurred in Camagüey province, and in Pinar del Río.

The entire Movement on the plains was now intensely preparing for a general revolutionary strike. The National Workers' Front organization (FON) had been constituted, but from the beginning it suffered from the sin of sectarianism. The workers reacted somewhat coolly to this organization, which came to life saturated completely with the spirit of the 26th of July and with ideas much too radical for the reality of the moment. Shortly before April 9, Fidel Castro issued a declaration seriously warning all who had not taken the path of the Revolution. Somewhat later, he issued another declaration to the workers, urging them to unite, inside or outside the FON, since he now saw that this organization alone could not promote a general strike.

Our troops threw themselves into the struggle, and Camilo Cienfuegos, then captain of the Fourth Column, descended to the plains of Oriente in the region of Bayamo, where death and confusion quickly were sown among the enemy. Finally, April 9 arrived and our struggle was in vain. The national leadership of the Movement, completely misunderstanding the principles of mass struggle, tried to initiate the strike without previous announcement, by surprise and sudden violence, thus losing complete support of the workers and resulting in the death of many great comrades throughout the country. April 9 was a resounding failure that at no time endangered the stability of the regime. Furthermore, after that tragic date, the government was able to move troops, sending them gradually to Oriente, to bring destruction to the Sierra Maestra. Our defense had to move even deeper into the Sierra Maestra. The government continued to increase the number of regiments in place against our positions, until the number of troops reached 10,000 men. With them the offensive was initiated on May 25 in the village of Las Mercedes, our advance position.

The combat ineffectiveness of Batista's army was demonstrated there—and also our scanty resources. Two hundred weapons against 10,000 weapons of all kinds was an enormous disadvantage. Our boys fought valiantly for two days, in a proportion of one against 10 or 15; fighting, besides, against mortars, tanks and aviation, until the small group had to abandon the village. It was commanded by Captain Angel Verdecia, who a month later would die heroically in combat.

At that time, Fidel Castro received a letter from the traitor, Eulogio Cantillo. As Operations Chief for the enemy—and true to his opportunist politics—Cantillo wrote the Rebel Chief telling him that the offensive would take place in any case, but that good care should be taken of "The Man" (Fidel) pending the final result of negotiations. The offensive did indeed take its course. In two and a half months of hard fighting the enemy lost more than a thousand men, including dead, wounded, prisoners and deserters. Left in our hands were 600 weapons, including a tank, 12 mortars, 12 tripod machine guns, 20-odd hand machine guns and an enormous number of automatic arms, besides a great quantity of ammunition and equipment of all kinds, as well as 450 prisoners who were handed over to the Red Cross at the end of the campaign.

The back of Batista's army was broken after this last offensive in the Sierra Maestra, but the Army was still not beaten. The struggle had to go on. The final strategy was then established, to attack in three places: Santiago de Cuba, to be subjected to a flexible encirclement; Las Villas, where I would have to go; and Pinar del Río, on the other end of the island, where Camilo Cienfuegos would go, as commander of Column Two—named for Antonio Maceo, to recall the historic campaign by that great leader in 1895 who in those epic days traversed the entire territory of Cuba as far as Mantua.[7] Camilo Cienfuegos would not complete the second part of his program, since the necessities of war forced him to remain in Las Villas.

When the regiments attacking the Sierra Maestra had been liquidated and the normal front restored, with the effectiveness and morale of our troops heightened, it was decided to begin the march to Las Villas, the central province. In the military order sent us, the principal strategic plan indicated was the systematic cutting of communications between the two extremes of the island. Further, I was ordered to establish relations with all political groups in the mountainous regions of that area and I was given ample powers to govern the zone under my military command. Marching under these instructions and expecting to arrive in four days, we departed by truck on August 30, 1958, but a freak accident delayed us. That night a small truck arrived, carrying uniforms and the gasoline necessary for the vehicles that were now ready, and a shipment of arms also arrived by air at an airport close to the road. Though the plane landed at night it was located by the enemy, and the airport was systematically bombed from 8:00 P.M. until 5 o'clock in the morning, when we burned the plane to prevent its falling into enemy hands or being bombed by day with even worse results. The enemy troops advanced on the airport and intercepted the truck with the gasoline, so that we had to go on foot. In this way we began the march on August 31 without trucks or horses, hoping to pick them up later on crossing the highway from Manzanillo to Bayamo. We did, in fact, find the trucks as expected, but on September 1 we were hit by a devastating hurricane that destroyed all transit routes except the Central Highway, the only paved road in that region of Cuba, obliging us to abandon our vehicles. From that time on, it was necessary to use horses or go on foot. We were equipped with sufficient ammunition, a bazooka with 40 projectiles, and everything necessary for a long journey and the rapid pitching of camp.

The succeeding days were difficult, though we were in the friendly territory of Oriente—crossing flooded rivers, striving constantly to keep dry our ammunition and the arms; looking for fresh horses to replace the exhausted ones; leaving populated areas as we moved further away from the eastern province.

We traversed difficult, flooded terrain, attacked by a plague of mosquitoes that made our hours of rest unbearable, eating little and badly, drinking from swampy rivers or simply swamps. Our days seemed to grow longer and longer and to become truly horrible. It was now a week since we had left camp, and our forces were in a weakened condition as we crossed the Jobabo river that borders the provinces of Camagüey and Oriente. This river had risen considerably like the ones we had already crossed and others still ahead. Also, our men were beginning to suffer for want of boots, and many went barefoot through the swamps of south Camagüey.

On the night of September 9, while entering the town of La Federal, our advance party fell into an enemy ambush and two of our courageous comrades were killed. But most unfortunate was the fact that we were located by enemy forces who from then on would never cease attacking us. After a short combat, the small garrison at La Federal surrendered, and we took four prisoners. We had to move on with great caution, since our route was by now approximately known to the planes. We arrived a day or two later at Laguna Grande, together with the force led by Camilo, much better equipped than ours. This place stands out in our memory for the extraordinary number of mosquitoes. It was absolutely impossible to rest without mosquito netting, and not all had it.

Those were days of fatiguing marches across desolate areas, with nothing but mud and water. We were hungry and thirsty, and we could barely move ahead; our legs felt like lead and our weapons weighed us down. We continued with horses left us by Camilo when he obtained trucks, but we had to leave the horses behind near the Marcareño sugar mill. The scouts who were to have been sent never arrived, so we set off on our own.

Our advance column ran into an enemy post at Cuatro Compañeros, and a long battle began. It was daybreak, and with considerable difficulty most of our men managed to take cover in the densest thicket in the area. But the army advanced on our flanks, and we were forced to fight hard to enable some of our stragglers to cross a railroad line and reach the woods. When planes located us, bombings began by B-26s, C-47s, the big C-3 observation planes and smaller planes over an area not more than 200 yards wide. After this, we retreated. One man had been killed by a bomb and several wounded, including Captain Silva who went through the rest of the invasion with a fractured shoulder.

The picture looked somewhat brighter the next day, when several of the stragglers appeared. We were able to reunite the entire troop, except for ten men who were to join Camilo's column and march with it to the northern front of Las Villas province (Yaguajay). In spite of many difficulties, we always received aid from the people in the countryside. Always we found someone to be our guide or scout, or to provide us with the necessary food to go on. Naturally, it was not the unanimous support that we had in Oriente, but always there were people who would help us. Sometimes, too, people would inform on us, and we would barely make it across a farm. This was not primarily a direct act against us by the peasants but rather the result of their living conditions. These people had become slaves of the farm owners; fearing the loss of their daily sustenance, they told their masters of our presence in the region. The farm owners were only too happy to pass this information on to the authorities.

One afternoon we heard a report over the radio by General Francisco Tabernilla Dolz. In killer-tones he announced the destruction of the "hordes led by Che Guevara," going into detail about the dead and wounded, even giving names—which were obtained when they captured our knapsacks after the disastrous encounter with enemy forces a few days earlier. All this was mixed with false information invented by Army Staff Headquarters. The false news of our deaths made the troops rather light-spirited. However, a mood of pessimism came creeping in. Hunger and thirst, fatigue, a feeling of helplessness in the face of the enemy encircling us more and more, and, above all, the terrible foot disease known in the countryside as *mazamorra*—which made each step taken by our soldiers intolerable torture—turned us into an army of shadows. It was difficult to keep going, extremely difficult. Day by day the physical condition of our troops deteriorated. We had food every other day, and not always then. There was nothing to ameliorate this state of misery.

The worst days were when we were surrounded near the Baraguá sugar mill, in infested swampland, without a drop of drinking water, constantly under attack from the air, without a single horse to take the weakest men to the inhospitable mountains, our shoes completely destroyed by the muddy sea water, plants cutting our bare feet. We were in a disastrous condition when we got out of that encircled area and made our way to the famous Trocha (line of fortification) from Júcaro to Morón—the historic scene of many fierce battles between the patriots and the Spaniards in the War of Independence. We hardly had time to recover slightly when another storm broke out, inclement weather set in, enemy attacks occurred or reports came of the enemy's presence, and we were once more on the march. Increasingly the troops grew exhausted and disheartened. However, when the situation was most tense, when the only way to keep the exhausted men going was by insults, rebuffs and pleadings of all kinds, a sight in the distance caused faces to brighten and filled the group with new hope. It was a blue patch in the west—the mountain range of Las Villas, which our men now saw for the first time.

From that moment, similar privations seemed much lighter, everything much easier. We evaded the last encirclement and swam the Júcaro river, crossing from Camagüey to Las Villas province. That, too, brightened our spirits. Two days later we were safely in the heart of the Trinidad-Sancti Spíritus range, ready to begin the next stage of the war. Our rest lasted only two days, for we needed immediately to continue our march forward in an attempt to prevent the elections scheduled for November 3. We had arrived in the mountainous region of Las Villas on October 16. Time was short, and the task enormous. Camilo was doing his part in the north, planting fear in the hearts of supporters of the dictatorship.

4

Guerrillas Fight On

Our first job when we arrived in the Sierra del Escambray was defined clearly: to harass the dictatorship's military apparatus, above all its communications. Our immediate objective was to prevent elections from taking place. But work was made difficult by the short time to elections and by disunity among revolutionary factions, which had led to internal fighting and resulted even in the loss of life.

We had to attack the neighboring villages to prevent elections from being held. We drew up plans to take, simultaneously, the cities of Cabaiguán, Fomento and Sancti Spíritus on the rich plains in the center of the island. Meanwhile, the small garrison at Güinía de Miranda, in the mountains, was taken, and later we attacked the post in Banao, but with poor results. The days preceding November 3, election day, were filled with extraordinary activity. Our columns mobilized in all directions, with the result that few voters in those areas cast ballots. Troops led by Camilo Cienfuegos in the northern part of the province paralyzed the electoral farce. In general, everything from the transport of Batista soldiers to the movement of merchandise came to a halt.

There was practically no voting in Oriente; in Camagüey, the percentage was a little higher; and in the west, despite everything, popular abstention from voting was notable. Abstention appeared in Las Villas spontaneously, as there had been no time to organize synchronized, passive mass resistance and guerrilla activities.

One battle after another took place in Oriente on the First and Second Fronts, and also on the Third where the Antonio Guiteras Column exerted pressure on Santiago de

Cuba, the provincial capital. Except for county seats, government in Oriente fell apart.

The situation was also growing serious in Las Villas as we stepped up attacks on communication lines.

On our arrival, we completely changed the system of struggle in the cities. We lost no time in transferring the best militiamen from the cities to the training camp for instruction in sabotage, a measure that proved effective in suburban areas.

In November and December of 1958 we gradually closed off the highways. Captain Silva completely cut off the Trinidad-Sancti Spíritus Highway, and the Central Highway was damaged seriously when the bridge over the Tuinicú River was partially destroyed. The central railway line was cut at several points and the southern line by the Second Front, while the northern line was cut by Camilo Cienfuegos' troops. And so the island was divided effectively.

The most turbulent area, Oriente, received government assistance by air and sea, in a highly precarious way. Signs of enemy deterioration were growing steadily.

We had to undertake an intensive campaign for revolutionary unity in the Escambray. In this region there was one group from the National Second Front of the Escambray, another from the Revolutionary Directorate (headed by Major Faure Chomón), another small group from the *Organización Auténtica,* another from the Popular Socialist Party[8] (headed by Torres), and ourselves. Thus, there were five separate organizations operating under different commands in the same province. Following lengthy conversations which I held with leaders of the various groups, a series of agreements were reached and we set about organizing a front more or less united.

After December 16, the systematic destruction of bridges and of all means of communication placed the dictatorship in a difficult situation to defend its outposts or even the Central Highway. At dawn that day, the Falcon River bridge on the Central Highway was destroyed and communications between Havana and the cities east of Santa Clara were practically all cut. Our forces surrounded and attacked a number of towns, the southernmost of which was Fomento. The commander of the garrison conducted a more or less efficient defense for several days, but despite aerial attacks against our Rebel Army, the demoralized land troops of the dictatorship did not advance in support of their comrades. Realizing the futility of resistance, the garrison surrendered, and more than 100 rifles were added to the liberation forces' supplies.

Without giving the enemy a chance to recover, we decided immediately to paralyze the Central Highway. On December 21, we simultaneously attacked Cambaiguán and Guayos, both on the Highway. Within a few hours the latter surrendered, and two days later the former, with its 90 soldiers, followed suit. (The garrisons surrendered on the understanding that the troops would go free, provided they abandon liberated territory. In that way they had the opportunity to surrender their weapons and save their lives.) In Cabaiguán we saw again the inefficiency of the dictatorship, which at no time sent in infantry reinforcements to back up the surrounded troops.

Camilo Cienfuegos took a number of small towns in the northern area of Las Villas and step by step surrounded Yaguajay, the last stronghold of the tyranny's troops. Their commander, a captain of Chinese background, resisted for 11 days, thus preventing the mobilization of revolutionary forces of the region while our men continued along the Central Highway, advancing toward the provincial capital of Santa Clara.

Cabaiguán fell, and we set our sights on Placetas. The latter surrendered after one day of fighting, with the active cooperation of members of the Revolutionary Directorate. After taking Placetas, we liberated in rapid succession Remedios and Caibarién (an important port on the northern coast). Things began to look grim for the dictatorship with the rebels winning constant victories in Oriente, the Second Front of the Escambray capturing small garrisons, and Camilo Cienfuegos controlling the north.

When the enemy withdrew from Camajuani without offering resistance, we were ready for the decisive assult on the capital of the province of Las Villas. (Santa Clara, the focal point of the island's central plain, has a population of 150,000 and is the nation's rail and communications nerve center. It is surrounded by small, barren rises that had been taken by Batista forces.)

At the time of the attack, our forces had augmented considerably their supply of weapons by taking several posts; we also had some heavy weapons, but they lacked ammunition. We had a bazooka without shells and we had to face a dozen enemy tanks. We realized that to fight effectively we had to reach the populated areas of the city, where the effectiveness of tanks is reduced drastically.

Troops from the Revolutionary Directorate were charged with taking rural guard outpost No. 31, and we concentrated on besieging nearly all the strong points of Santa Clara. Basically, however, our struggle was directed against troops defending an armored train located at the entrance to the Camajuani road. The Army tenaciously defended its position with excellent weapons in comparison to our own.

On December 29 we began the battle. At first we used the university as our base of operations. Next we set up headquarters closer to the center of the city. Our forces fought against troops supported by armored units, routing them. Many of our men paid for their daring with their lives; the dead and wounded filled improvised cemeteries and hospitals.

I recall an incident that demonstrates the spirit of our forces in those days. I had reprimanded a soldier for sleeping out a battle, and he replied that he had been disarmed for having fired a shot at an unpropitious moment. I had replied dryly, "Get another rifle by going into the battle unarmed—if you are man enough to do it."

Later, at Santa Clara, when I was cheering up the wounded in a makeshift hospital, a dying man touched me and said, "Remember me, Major? You sent me to get a gun at Remedios—and I got one here." It was the man who had accidentally fired his gun at the wrong moment. He died a few minutes later, content to have demonstrated his bravery. That is what our Rebel Army is like.

The enemy was firmly entrenched in the Capiro hills. We fought there the entire day of December 30. We were also taking gradually various points in the city. At that time, communications were cut between the center of Santa Clara and the armored train. Its occupants, seeing themselves surrounded in the Capiro hills, tried to escape over the stretch of tracks that we had previously torn up. The engine and several cars were derailed. The battle changed form, and the occupants of the train were flushed out with Molotov cocktails. They had been magnificently protected, although only willing to fight at a safe distance, from comfortable positions and against an opponent practically defenseless, much the same way as the colonists had fought the Indians in the West of the United States. With our men throwing Molotov cocktails from nearby points and from railroad cars, the train covered by protective sheet-metal plates became a veritable oven for the soldiers within. In a few hours, the entire body had surrendered, with 22 cars of anti-aircraft guns, machine guns and a fabulous amount of ammunition—fabulous in comparison to our scanty supplies.

We had taken the electric power plant and the entire northwest section of the city. We announced over the radio that Santa Clara was almost entirely in the hands of the Revolution. In that report, which I issued as Commander-in-Chief of the Armed Forces in Las Villas, I had the sad duty of telling the Cuban people of the death of Captain Roberto Rodríguez, nicknamed "The Cowboy," young leader of the "Suicide Squad" who had flirted with death a thousand and one times in the struggle for liberation. The

"Suicide Squad" was a model of revolutionary morale; it was composed only of specially selected volunteers. Whenever one of the men died—and that happened in every battle—and a replacement was selected, those rejected showed deep disappointment, even grief. It was strange to see these brave, battle-hardened veterans showing their youth by tears at not having been selected for the first line in combat and death.

Later the police station fell, with the surrender of the tanks defending it. In rapid succession outpost No. 31 surrendered to Major Cubela, while the jail, the courthouse, the headquarters of the provincial government and the Grand Hotel fell to our forces. On the tenth floor of the latter snipers continued shooting almost to the end of the battle.

The only remaining stronghold was the Leoncio Vidal Garrison, the largest fortress in central Cuba.

It was already January 1, 1959, and there were symptoms of growing weakness among the defending forces. On the morning of that day we sent Captains Nuñez Jiménez and Rodríguez de la Vega to receive the formal surrender of the garrison. The news was both contradictory and extraordinary. That day, Batista had fled and the leadership of his armed forces had fallen apart. Our two delegates established radio contact with Cantillo, inviting him to surrender, but he stated he could not accept the offer because it constituted an ultimatum. He announced he had taken over command of the army following precise instructions of Fidel Castro. We immediately made contact with Fidel and reported the news to him, giving our opinion that Cantillo's attitude was traitorous; his opinion coincided with ours. (During these decisive moments Cantillo allowed all the responsible figures of the Batista government to flee. His attitude was the more unfortunate considering that he was an officer who had made contact with us and whom we trusted as a military man of honor.)

The following events are familiar to all: Castro's refusal

to recognize Cantillo, and his order to march on the city of
Havana; Colonel Barquín's taking over as army chief after
leaving the Isle of Pines prison; the taking of Camp
Columbia by Camilo Cienfuegos and of La Cabaña fortress
by our Column Eight; and within a few days, the final
installation of Fidel Castro as Prime Minister of the provisional government. All this belongs to the country's
present political history.

Now [July 1959] we hold a position in which we are much
more than actors in the history of one nation; at this
moment we are the hope of unredeemed America. All eyes,
whether of the big oppressors or of the hopeful, are fixed
upon us. The development of the people's movements in
America depends to a great extent upon our future attitude
and on our ability to solve manifold problems. Every step
we take is closely watched by the omnipresent eyes of the
big oppressors and by the optimistic eyes of our brothers
of America.

With our feet firmly on the ground, we are setting to
work to produce the first fruits of the Revolution, and
coming up against the first difficulties. But is not Cuba's
fundamental problem the same faced by all America—huge
Brazil with its millions of square miles, a land of wonders
that is a continent in itself? Monoproduction. In Cuba we
are the slaves of sugar cane, the umbilical cord that ties us
to the great northern market. We must diversify our farm
production, stimulate industry and guarantee suitable
markets, accessible through our own transportation system,
for our agricultural and mining products—and our industrial
products as well, in the not too distant future.

The government's first great battle will be the Agrarian
Reform. It will be daring and inclusive, but flexible. It will
destroy the latifundium in Cuba, but not Cuban means of
production. This battle will absorb a good share of the
strength of the people and the government during the
coming years. Land will be given free to the peasant, and
anyone who shows he owns his land honorably will be

paid in long-term bonds. In addition, the peasants will be given technical aid, farm products will have guaranteed markets and production will be channeled so as to benefit the nation. The great battle for Agrarian Reform will allow Cuba's incipient industries, within a short time, to compete with the huge industries of countries where capitalism has reached its highest level of development. The Agrarian Reform will be achieved along with the creation of a new domestic market; the distribution of new products to satisfy an incipient market will lead to the necessity of exporting some products, and we will need a suitable means of delivering them to various parts of the world. This means a merchant fleet, as already provided in the Maritime Development Law. With these elemental weapons, we Cubans will undertake the struggle for complete liberation of our soil. We know it will not be easy, but all are conscious of the enormous historic responsibility of the 26th of July Movement, of the Cuban Revolution, of the nation in general, to provide an example for all the peoples of America whom we must not disappoint.

Our friends from the unbowed continent can rest assured that, if necessary, we will fight to the last economic consequence of our acts. And if the battle is carried still further, we will fight to the last drop of our rebel blood to make this land a sovereign Republic, with the genuine attributes of a nation that is happy and democratic and a true brother to the other peoples of Latin America.

REFERENCE NOTES

1. On July 26, 1953, an armed group led by Fidel Castro stormed the Moncada barracks in Santiago de Cuba, and was repulsed after bloody fighting. This action is considered as opening the path to armed struggle; the July 26th Movement takes its name from the date of that event.

2. Díaz Tamayo was a general in Batista's army.

3. Reference here is to differences over the tactics of the general strike of April 9. *See* pp. 124-25.

4. Herbert Matthews, correspondent of the *New York Times;* his articles appeared in the *Times* on February 24, 25 and 26, 1957.

5. The Orthodox party, a middle-class liberal party, opposed the Batista dictatorship; many young people under its influence joined the July 26th Movement. Chibás was its leader; *see* Note 15.

6. The invasion of Playa Girón, on "the Bay of Pigs," was carried out by Cuban exiles under the auspices of the Central Intelligence Agency, and with the knowledge of President Kennedy. On April 17, 1961, Havana was bombed. The invasion itself began on April 19, and within 72 hours met with complete defeat.

7. The Students' Directorate has been the center of revolutionary student activity at the University of Havana since the days of the Machado regime.

8. Hubert Matos, a major in the Rebel Army, turned against the Revolution after its victory. He is presently in jail for conspiring to overthrow the government.

9. Felipe Pazos, of the Orthodox party, was an economist at the University of Havana and a liberal opponent of both the Machado and Batista dictatorships. When the revolution came to power, he soon deserted Cuba to become a consultant for the Organization of American States and the Alliance for Progress.

10. Pardo Llado and Conte Agüero were popular radio commentators and journalists who went against the Revolution.

11. Gerardo Machado, who became President of Cuba in 1925, was forced to resign in 1933 when a general strike and loss of army support forced him to flee. A provisional government, headed by Carlos Manuel de Céspedes was chosen but lasted only one month, when it was overthrown by a student coup, which installed Ramón Grau San Martín in the presidency. Grau was in turn removed from office four months later by the "sergeants' coup" led by Fulgencio Batista.

12. Manuel Urrutia resigned from the provisional presidency after almost a year in office when the land reform and other social measures of the Revolutionary government, of which Fidel Castro was Prime Minister, challenged his own upper class loyalties.

13. Prío Socarrás, leader of the Autentico party and President of Cuba from 1948 to 1952, was overthrown by the military coup of March 10, 1952, which began the second Batista dictatorship.

14. The Beatón family continued counter-revolutionary activity after the founding of the Castro government.

15. Eddie Chibás was president of the Orthodox party and, after his suicide, his brother Raúl succeeded him. The latter, together with Felipe Pazos, came to the Sierra for a conference with Fidel Castro.

16. *Diario de la Marina,* controlled by the Jesuits, was the most reactionary newspaper in Cuba.

17. On October 15, 1957, a number of anti-Batista groups met in Miami and formed the Council of Cuban Liberation. Its manifesto called for a provisional government and the restoration of the 1940 Constitution. Among the participants were Prío Socarrás of the Autentico party, Felipe Pazos of the Orthodox party who also claimed to speak for Fidel Castro, and representatives of the Federation of University Students, the Revolutionary Directorate, the *Organización Auténtica* and the Revolutionary Workers' Directorate.

18. Signed in the Venezuelan capital on July 20, 1958, the Caracas Pact proclaimed three central aims: a general strike in Cuba, a provisional government, and general elections as soon as possible. Among the signatories were Enrique Rodríguez of the Revolutionary Directorate, Manuel Bisbe of the Orthodox party, and for the Autenticos, Prío Socarrás and Antonio de Varona (who later was to head the Washington sponsored "provisional government" at the time of the "Bay of Pigs" invasion). Although the sponsors claimed the support of Fidel Castro, he denounced the Pact.

19. The August 1957 strike was a spontaneous outpouring in protest against the assassination of Frank País by Batista henchmen on the street in Santiago de Cuba.

20. This article is published posthumously and is taken from *Granma,* English Edition, November 12, 1967. It was written in October 1964, but Che refused to permit its publication until he had reworked parts of it.

21. The "tragic day of April 9" refers to the failure of the general strike of that date. *See* pp. 124-25.

22. Reference here is to the invasion of the plains by the Rebel Army, which culminated in the victory of the Revolution. *See* pp. 133 *ff.*

23. The plane on which Camilo Cienfuegos was traveling to Havana disappeared *en route* and was never found.

FOUR ARTICLES ON THE REVOLUTIONARY WAR

1. The reference here is to the "mediation" undertaken by U.S. Ambassador Sumner Welles when it became apparent that the Machado tyranny was no longer useful to U.S. interests. In the midst of a nation-wide popular movement against the dictator, Welles sought a formula that would substitute for the Machado regime a moderate government able to keep the opposition within safe bounds. However, Machado was overthrown on August 3, 1933, by a national general strike, in which the Communist Party and the unions organized by it played a leading role.

2. The Platt Amendment, framed by Senator Orville Platt of Connecticut as a rider to the Army Appropriations Bill of 1901, stipulated the conditions of U.S. intervention in Cuba, and practically made Cuba a U.S. protectorate. The amendment was forced into the Cuban Constitution and into a perma-

nent treaty between the U.S. and Cuba. It served as the basis for intervention in 1906, 1912, 1917 and 1920, and was finally abrogated in 1934.

3. Narciso López, a former general in the Spanish army, sought to achieve Cuba's independence from Spain with the support of annexationist elements in the United States. On his third invasion attempt, in 1851, he landed in Cuba but was soon captured and publicly garroted.

4. Alberto Bayó, a general in the Spanish Republican army, went to Mexico after the Spanish Civil War. There he met Fidel and Raúl Castro and became the military instructor of the *Granma* group. After the Revolution, General Bayó came to Cuba where he served as instructor to the Cuban armed forces until his death in 1967.

5. The name Alegría de Pío is "paradoxical" because in the literal sense *alegría* may mean "merriment" or "rejoicing" and *pío*, the "pious" or the "devout."

6. The Cuban revolutionists were called "Mambi" by the Spanish colonialists, as a term of derision, but it was taken over by the Cubans themselves. The wars of 1868 and 1895 were the First and the Second Wars of Independence.

7. Antonio Maceo, a Negro, was the great Cuban military leader, who rose from the rank of corporal to general during his leadership of the brilliant guerrilla campaigns against the Spaniards, in the Ten Years' War of 1868-78 and in 1895.

8. Popular Socialist Party was the name assumed by the Cuban Communists during the first Batista regime.

BIOGRAPHICAL NOTES

ACUÑA, MANUEL. Guerrilla veteran.

ACUÑA, VILO. Nephew of Manuel Acuña; guerrilla Major.

ACUÑA, SERGIO. In early guerrilla group, deserter.

ALARCÓN, JUVENTINO. Guerrilla recruit from Manzanillo, killed in action.

ALMEIDA, JUAN. *Granma* veteran and guerrilla Major; commander of Column Three; now head of Cuban Army

ALMEIDA, TUTO. Peasant guide.

AMEIJEIRAS, EFIGENIO. *Granma* veteran, guerrilla Major.

ARBENTOSA. Arrived on *Granma*, wounded at Alegría de Pío.

BANDERAS. Guerrilla Lieutenant, killed in action.

BARRERAS, COL. Batista's chief of operations against Rebel Army in Sierra Maestra.

BEATÓN, PUPO AND MANOLO. Brothers with guerrillas, turned against revolution.

BENÍTEZ. In *Granma* group.

CABRERA, EMILIO. Peasant, helped guerrillas.

CÁCERAS VALLE, JULIO ROBERTO ("El Patojo"). Guatemalan, friend of Che, killed in action in his country.

CALDERO, HERMES. Guerrilla Major.

CANTILLO, EULOGIO. Batista's Chief of Operations in last offensive against Sierra Maestra; took over command of Army when Batista fled.

CAPOTE, GILBERTO. Ex-army man, joined guerrillas; killed in action.

CASILLAS, MAJOR. Commander of Batista troops in region of Sierra Maestra.

CASTRO MERCADER, RAÚL. *Granma* veteran, guerrilla Major, leader of

Column Six; now Minister of Defense.

CHAÓ. A Spanish Civil War veteran, in *Granma* group.

CHOMÓN, FAURE. Member of Student Directorate; took part in attempt on Batista's life in 1957; guerrilla leader in Escambray; after Revolution, Cuban Ambassador to USSR.

CIENFUEGOS, CAMILO. *Granma* veteran, on Fidel Castro's general staff, Captain in Che's Column Four in invasion of Las Villas province; killed in airplane accident after Revolution.

CRESPO, LUIS. *Granma* veteran, guerrilla Major, on Fidel's general staff in Sierra Maestra.

CRUCITO. Guerrilla fighter and balladeer, killed in action.

CUERVO NAVARRO, PELAYO. Orthodox party leader, murdered by Batista henchmen.

DE LA VEGA, RODRÍGUEZ. Guerrilla Captain.

DEL VALLE, SERGIO. Guerrilla doctor, promoted to Major.

DÍAZ, EPIFANIO. Landowner whose sons joined guerrillas, his house was contact place.

DÍAZ, JULITO. Moncada and *Granma* veteran, killed at El Uvero.

DÍAZ, NANO. Guerrilla, killed at El Uvero.

DÍAZ, RAÚL. *Granma* veteran.

DOMÍNGUEZ, GUILLERMO. A leader of Manzanillo guerrilla recruits, killed in action.

ECHEVERRÍA. With early group of guerrillas.

ECHEVERRÍA, JOSÉ ANTONIO. Student leader, killed in attempt on Batista's life in 1957.

ELÍAS, MELQUIADES. Peasant, helped *Granma* group.

EL VAQUERITO. *See* Rodríguez, Roberto.

EMILIANO. Peasant, sheltered and fed guerrillas.

ESPÍN, VILMA. Leader of July 26th Movement in cities, Raúl Castro's wife; after Revolution became President of Federation of Cuban Women.

FAJARDO, MANUEL. Guerrilla Major, on Fidel's General Staff in Sierra Maestra.

FAJARDO, PITI. Guerrilla doctor killed in Escambray.

FERNÁNDEZ, MARCELO. A coordinator of July 26th Movement; vice-president of National Bank.

FRÍAS, CIRO. Local merchant who joined guerrillas, killed in battle.

GARCÍA, GUILLERMO. Guerrilla veteran, after Revolution became chief of Army of Western Sector.

GONZÁLEZ, CÁNDIDO. *Granma* group, killed after landing.

GUERRA, ARÍSTEDES. Contact for food transport.

GUERRA, EUTEMIO. Guide for *Granma* group, turned traitor and was executed.

HART, ARMANDO. July 26th Movement leader; now Organizational Secretary of Cuban Communist Party.

HERMES. Son of the peasant Emiliano, served as guerrilla guide.

HERMO. A leader of Manzanillo guerrilla recruits.

IGLESIAS, JOEL. Young guerrilla fighter, later President of Rebel Youth and Major in Rebel Army.

IGLESIAS ("Marcos," "Nicaragua"). Leader of July 26th Movement in Santiago de Cuba; after Revolution, Governor of Las Villas.

JIMÉNEZ, NUNEZ. Guerrilla Captain.

LABRADA, EMILIO. Young peasant, joined guerrillas.

LAMOTTE, HUMBERTO. Arrived on *Granma*, killed at Alegría de Pío.

LEYVA, HERMES. Guerrilla, killed at El Hombrito.

LÓPEZ, ENRIQUE. Boyhood friend of Castros, contact man for guerrillas.

LÓPEZ, "NICO." *Granma* group, killed after landing.

MACEO. Guerrilla Lieutenant, murdered while on mission to Santiago.

MÁRQUEZ, JUAN MANUEL. *Granma* group, killed after landing.

MENDOZA, ELIGIO. Guerrilla guide, killed at El Uvero.

MERCADER, CASERO. Guerrilla Lieutenant.

MOLL. Guerrilla, killed at El Uvero.

MONTANÉ. Arrived in *Granma*.

MORA, BENITO. Peasant, helped guerrillas.

MORA, MEMELAO. Killed in attempt on Batista's life in 1957.

MORA, VÍCTOR. Guerrilla, killed at El Uvero.

MORALES, CALIXTO. *Granma* veteran and poet.

MORÁN, "GALLEGO." In first guerrilla forces; deserted and later turned traitor.

MOSQUERA, SÁNCHEZ. Commander of Batista troops in Sierra.

MOTOLÁ. In early guerrilla group.

NARANJO, CRISTINO. Guerrilla Major, murdered by Beatón brothers.

NICOLÁS. Ex-army man, joined guerrillas.

NODA. Guerrilla Lieutenant, killed in action.

OÑATE. ALEJANDRO ("Cantinflas"). Guerrilla Lieutenant.

ORESTES. Guerrilla Lieutenant.

PAÍS, FRANK. Leader of July 26th Movement in Santiago de Cuba;

PAÍS, FRANK (*cont.*) murdered by Batista henchmen in 1957.

PAÍS, JOSUÉ. Frank's brother; killed in Santiago.

PARDO, ISRAEL. Guerrilla Captain.

PAULINO. Medical assistant to Che.

PAZOS, JAVIER. Translator, joined guerrillas.

PENA. Student recruit, became a guerrilla Major.

PÉREZ, CRESCENCIO. Veteran guerrilla leader.

PÉREZ, FAUSTINO. *Granma* veteran, worked with Movement in the cities.

PÉREZ, IGNACIO. Guerrilla Captain, son of Crescensio, killed in action.

PÉREZ, JULIO. Guerrilla fighter.

PESANT, ROBERTO. Leader of guerrilla recruits from Manzanillo.

PONCE. In *Granma* group.

RAMOS LATOUR, RENÉ. Guerrilla Major, killed in action.

REDONDO, CIRO. *Granma* veteran, guerrilla Major on Fidel's general staff in Sierra Maestra.

RIVERO, PEDRO. Guerrilla, killed at Bueycito.

RODRÍGUEZ, ARMANDO. Came on *Granma*, deserter.

RODRÍGUEZ, FRUCTUOSO. Student, took part in attempt on Batista's life in 1957.

RODRÍGUEZ, ROBERTO ("The Cowboy"). Guerrilla Captain, leader of "Suicide Squad," killed at Santa Clara.

RODRÍGUEZ, WILLIAM. Guerrilla Lieutenant.

SABORIT, EVILIO. Guerrilla, later a Major in Rebel Army.

SÁNCHEZ, CALIXTO. Leader of the Autentico party guerrilla expedition.

SÁNCHEZ, CELIA. July 26th Movement leader, joined guerrillas in Sierra Maestra.

SÁNCHEZ, UNIVERSO. *Granma* veteran; on Fidel's general staff in Sierra Maestra.

SANTAMARÍA, HAYDÉE. Leader of July 26th Movement, Armando Hart's wife; now Vice-President of the Organization of Latin American Solidarity (OLAS).

SMITH, JUAN. *Granma* group, killed after landing.

SOSA, MEROB. Major of Batista army.

SOTO, "PEDRÍN." A *Granma* veteran, killed in action.

SOTOMAYOR. Three brothers, in early guerrilla group.

SOTÚS, JORGE. Captain of Manzanillo guerrilla recruits; later turned against the Revolution.

SUÁREZ, RAÚL. In *Granma* group, wounded at Alegría de Pío.

TABERNILLA DOLZ, FRANCISCO. On Batista's General Staff.

TAMAYO, PANCHO. Peasant, guerrilla contact man; killed by counter-revolutionists.

TORRES. Communist (PSP) guerrilla leader in Escambray.

TORRES, SINECIO. Guerrilla guide, deserted.

VALDÉS, RAMIRO. Moncada and *Granma* veteran, guerrilla Major; Minister of the Interior in Revolutionary Government.

VERDECIA, ANGEL. Guerrilla Captain, killed in action.

WESTBROOK, JOE. Student, took part in attempt on Batista's life in 1957.

ZENÓN ACOSTA, JULIO. Peasant who joined guerrillas, killed by Batista troops.